HOW TO INVEST
IN
SHARES & MUTUAL FUNDS

ABOUT THE AUTHORS

Dr. L.C. Gupta is Director, Society for Capital Market Research & Development. He was formerly Member, SEBI and Chairman of its Derivatives Committee, and also Member of several other committees, like RBI's Advisory Council to Board for Financial Supervision, High Powered Committee on Stock Exchanges, Technical Study Group on Depository System and director on many company boards. He was Professor of Commerce at Delhi School of Economics; Director of Research at IFMR, Chennai; Chair Professor in Finance at XLRI, and Dean (Research) at MDI, Gurgaon. His research studies have been published by Clarendon Press (U.K.), Oxford University Press and Macmillans.

Naveen Kumar Jain is M.Com, M.Phil from Delhi School of Economics. He is Associate Professor in Commerce, Hans Raj College, Delhi University. He has co-authored several research publications of SCMRD. He is a keen nature and wildlife photographer.

HOW TO INVEST IN SHARES & MUTUAL FUNDS

— A BASIC BOOK FOR INVESTORS —

by

Dr. L.C. Gupta
Formerly Member of SEBI

&

Naveen Jain
Associate Professor in Commerce
Hans Raj College, University of Delhi

Kaveri Books
New Delhi - 110 002

ISBN : 978-81-7479-116-0
First Published in 2011
This Edition 2016

Published by
Kaveri Books
4832/24, Ansari Road, Darya Ganj
New Delhi-110002 (India)
Tel: 011-23288140, 47072321
E-mail : info@kaveribooks.com
kaveribooks@gmail.com
Website : www.kaveribooks.com

Typeset in Palatino by
Aarati Computers, New Delhi

PRINTED IN INDIA

Foreword

I am happy to note that the Society for Capital Market Research & Development has brought out a basic book to help and guide ordinary investors in understanding the working of the stock market.

Glancing through the contents, I am impressed by the care taken to cover the various important aspects which are of relevance to the ordinary investors.

The book fills a real need as there is presently no such book for the Indian investors. It will help investors to choose the right companies in which to invest and to adopt the right strategies for investing in shares without taking undue risk, keeping in view one's financial circumstances and family responsibilities.

The book provides useful insights about the market's behaviour over both long-term and short term. I am sure that the ordinary investors would find the book extremely useful.

Dr. Abid Hussain
Chairman
Society for Capital Market
Research & Development

Contents

List of Tables

List of Charts

Acronyms

ADRs	American Depository Receipts
ASBA	Applications Supported by Blocked Amount
B/S	Balance Sheet
BSE	Bombay Stock Exchange
CDSL	Central Depository Services Limited
CRA	Credit Rating Agency
CRISIL	Credit Rating and Information Services of India Limited
DP	Depository Participants
EPS	Earning Per Share
ETFs	Exchange-traded funds
FIIs	Foreign Institutional Investors
GDP	Gross Domestic Product
GDRs	Global Depository Receipts
ICRA	Investment Information and Credit Rating Agency of India Limited
IDBI	The Industrial Development Bank of India
IDRs	Indian Depository Receipts
IPOs	Initial Public Offers
OTC Market	Over-the-counter market
NAV	Net Asset Value
NASD	National Association of Securities Dealers (of U.S)
NASDAQ	National Association of Securities Dealers Automated Quotation (of U.S)

NSDL	National Securities Depository Limited
NSE	National Stock Exchange of India
PAT	Profit-after-Tax
PBT	Profit-before-Tax
P& L A/c	Profit and Loss Account
QIB	Qualified Institutional Buyers
SEBI	Securities & Exchange Board of India
SEC	Securities Exchange Commission (of U.S.)
Sensex	Sensitive Index of Bombay Stock Exchange
SIP	Systematic Investment Plan
UTI	Unit Trust of India

SOCIETY FOR CAPITAL MARKET RESEARCH AND DEVELOPMENT

Established in October 1989 under the Societies Registration Act, Delhi, the Society is a non-profit research institution. It has published several major research studies and surveys carried out in collaboration with the regulatory and operating institutions.

The Society has also been supported by contributions towards its endowment/Corpus Fund by UTI, ICICI, IDBI and HDFC, as also by a capital grant from the Indian Government.

Its Board of Governors comprises:

- Dr. Abid Hussain (Chairman)
- Dr. Abad Ahmed
- Mr. Chandra Mohan
- Mr. C.K. Hazari
- Dr. D.B. Gupta
- Mr. A.P. Gandhi
- Dr. D.H. Pai Panadiker (treasurer)
- Mr. P.G. Mankad
- Dr. Nitish Sengupta
- Mr. M.S. Verma
- Mr. Jagdish Baijal and
- Dr. L.C. Gupta (Director & Member-Secretary)

LIST OF PUBLICATIONS

1. Indian Shareowners: A Survey (1991)
2. Stock Exchange Trading in India: Agenda for Reform (1992)
3. Mutual Funds and Asset Preference: Household Survey (1993)
4. Shareowners' Geographic Distribution (1994)
5. The Roots of India's Stock Market Crisis, 1995-97
6. Indian Stock Market P/E Rations (1998)
7. India's Financial Markets & Institutions (1999)
8. Returns on Indian Equity Shares (2000)
9. Indian Households' Investment Preferences (2001)
10. How Good are Mutual Funds: The Household Investors' Perceptions (2001)
11. India's Stock Market & Household Investors 2001-04
12. Indian Share Buyback Practices & Their Regulation (2006)
13. The Changing Investment Preferences of Indian Households (2008)

1

Introduction

Need for a book for ordinary investors:

1.1 There is no book in India to help the ordinary investors in understanding the basics of investing in shares and mutual funds. This is an important reason why only a minute percentage of Indian households invest in the stock market.

1.2 We are not advocating that the ordinary investors should speculate or gamble in the share market. We want them to invest more intelligently, more cautiously and more profitably. All this is possible.

1.3 The present book is intended to fill the gap mentioned above. It deals with important aspects, such as how to identify the right companies, how much should one diversify the share portfolio, what should be the appropriate holding period, how to safeguard against the market's uncertain behaviour, etc., etc.

Understand the equity market's characteristics:

1.4 It needs to be noted that equity markets are typically characterized by much short-term turbulence, superimposed on long-term trends. Over the long-term, investing in shares can be quite rewarding. Investors need to be aware of the market`s behaviour so that they are prepared mentally and financially for all eventualities. Both rewards and risks need to be understood and properly balanced, keeping in view one`s personal and family circumstances.

Analytical tools:

1.5 There are important tools and techniques for analysing equity investments. We shall be explaining these. An important one is the P/E ratio, i.e. the ratio of price-per-share to earning-per-share. The investor needs to understand the various tools. They can be very helpful in deciding in which companies to invest and when. This will enable the investor to invest more intelligently and profitably.

IPOs vis-à-vis existing shares:

1.6 A choice before an equity investor is that he may buy existing shares from the market or he may invest in Initial Public Offers (i.e. IPOs). He has to weigh the relative advantages. The market for IPOs in India has undergone a fundamental change recently as a result of the system of compulsory grading. Such grading is unique to India. It has some serious shortcomings which have to be kept in mind in order to guard against pitfalls.

The Demat System:

1.7. An important market reform in India has been the creation of the Securities Depository System. This has done away with the old system of physical paper certificates. The certificates have been dematerialized. Hence, it is known as demat system. The paper-based system was not only costly for the investors but also had many irritating problems, such as certificates being lost in transit, or stolen or mutilated. We shall explain how the depository system operates.

Other aspects:

1.8 A separate chapter has been devoted to investing through mutual fund schemes. There is a great variety of such schemes. They are generally safer than investing in individual shares. Of course, investing in mutual funds is not as tempting and challenging as direct investing in shares. The investor has to consider whether to invest in shares directly or through mutual fund schemes or through both. We shall examine the main types of mutual fund schemes and the related regulatory system.

1.9 The final chapter is concerned with explaining the main accounting statements, viz., the Income Statement and the Balance Sheet. Investors need to understand and interpret these statements in order to judge how well a company is doing.

1.10 A Glossary at the end of the book briefly explains the terminology relating to the securities market.

2

Some Basic Financial Concepts Regarding Share Investment

Understanding the market's terminology:

2.1 The concepts explained in this chapter provide a necessary foundation in regard to investment in shares. In a sense, they are part and parcel of the market's language.

The EPS:

2.2 The value of a company's shares greatly depends on earnings per share (EPS). The EPS is arrived at simply by dividing the latest year's total earnings by the total number of shares. If the EPS of Company X is much more than that of Company Y, the shares of Company X will ordinarily be valued much higher than those of Company Y. Of course, the quality of EPS (specially its riskiness and likely future growth) will also have to be taken into account.

The P/E Ratio:

2.3 Whether the price of the particular shares is reasonable or not can be judged from the ratio of price-to-earnings, i.e., the P/E Ratio. It is the *ratio of the current market price of a share to the latest 12 months earnings-per-share (EPS).* The P/E ratios of individual companies are reported in the financial dailies (such as *The Economic Times*) along with share prices, covering the previous closing price, day's opening and closing prices, the day's highest and lowest prices, trading volume and also the number of trades. All this information can throw light on various aspects, such as the degree of liquidity as also price volatility of the various shares. Some shares may be highly liquid and can be easily sold or bought. Some may be very illiquid. An investor has to take into account all those aspects.

2.4 It may be observed from Table 2.1 that the P/E ratios have an amazingly wide range. For example, the P/E ratios of the 30 Sensex companies are found to range from 11.2 to 35.9 and of the 50 Nifty companies from 8.7 to 64.6. This is because the quality of the EPS varies among the individual companies, as we have mentioned a little earlier.

Table 2.1[1]

P/E RATIOS OF SENSEX AND NIFTY COMPANIES

Name of Company (1)	*P E Ratio* (2)	*Name of Company* (3)	*P E Ratio* (4)
SENSEX	**24.08**	**NIFTY**	**25.44**
Reliance Indus	19.5	Reliance Indus	19.5
Infosys Tech	28.2	Infosys Tech	28.1
ICICI Bank	31.2	ICICI Bank	31.3
Larsen & Turbo	35.8	Larsen & Turbo	35.8
HDFC	35.9	HDFC	35.8
HDFC Bank	35.6	HDFC Bank	35.6
ITC	31.0	ITC	31.0
SBI	16.5	SBI	16.6
ONGC	19.0	ONGC	19.0
Bharti Airtel	16.4	Bharti Airtel	16.4
Tata Consult	25.2	Tata Consult	25.2
BHEL	28.3	BHEL	28.3
Tata Steel	28.9	Axis Bank	23.8
Tata Motors	13.2	Tata Steel	29.0
Hind. Uniliver	29.9	Tata Motors	13.2
M& M	18.7	Hind. Uniliver	29.9
Jindal Steel P	19.1	IDFC	26.6
Hindalco	20.6	M& M	18.7
Sterlite Indus	14.5	Jindal Steel	19.1
Wipro	22.9	Hindalco	20.6
Tata Power	19.7	Sterlite Indus	14.5
Maruti Suzuki	18.1	Wipro	22.9
NTPC	21.2	Bajaj Auto	61.6
Reliance Infra	24.6	Tata Power	19.7
Hero Honda	16.5	GAIL	18.2
Cipla	24.2	Maruti Suzuki	18.1
Jaiprakash Asso	16.6	NTPC	21.2
DLF	37.1	Kotak Mah. Bk	27.3
Reliance Communications	11.2	Punjab National Bank	10.0
ACC	13.4	Reliance Infra	24.6
		Hero Honda	16.6
		Cipla	24.2
		Jaiprakash Asso	16.6
		Sun Pharma	24.1
		Dr. Reddy`s Lab	81.6
		Sesa Goa Unitech	8.7
		Cairn	50.1

Continued on next page....

1. Based on ET of 8th October, 2010

Name of Company (1)	*P E Ratio (2)*	*Name of Company (3)*	*P E Ratio (4)*
		DLF	37.1
		SAIL	14.2
		Siemens	38.0
		Reliance Communications	11.2
		Ambuja Cement	15.3
		ACC	13.5
		Rel Capital	58.1
		BPCL	—
		HCL Techno	27.7
		Ranbaxy Lab.	15.7
		Power Grid	20.9
		Reliance Power	64.6
		Suzlon Energy	—

Source : The Economic Times, 8th October, 2010

2.5 A relatively high P/E ratio may or may not be justified depending on the expected future growth of EPS. If the EPS is expected to grow relatively fast, such as doubling, tripling or even more over the next few years, the share price too would rise, resulting in capital gain for the shareholders.

The theoretical model:

2.6 Really speaking, the P/E ratio is a simple short-cut method for judging the prevailing price. According to the *theoretical model, the present value of a share depends on the expected future cash flows by way of dividends for the next, say, 5-10 years, discounted at the appropriate rate. The present value of the share is given by the following equation:*

$$\text{Present value} = \frac{D1}{(1+r)} + \frac{D2}{(1+r)} + \ldots \frac{Dn}{(1+r)^n} \quad \text{where:}$$

D1, D2....are year-to-year cash dividends; and Dn is the terminal price on sale of the investment at the end of year 'n` and 'r` is the appropriate discount rate which takes into account the prevailing rates.

2.7 The investor has to judge what level of P/E ratio can be regarded as reasonable in a given case, taking into account the future prospects of the particular company, as also the P/E ratios of comparable companies.

2.8 **Inter-company differences:** As we have pointed out earlier, the P/E ratio differs widely among companies. This is because of differing future prospects specially with respect to the expected growth rate of earnings and also because of differences in the perceived quality and reputation of the various company managements. Within an industry, those companies whose managements command greater confidence of investors would usually have a relatively higher P/E ratio.

Market's average P/E Ratio:

2.9 Apart from the P/E ratios of individual companies, the P/E ratio for the market as a whole should also be taken into account. It is indicative of the generally prevailing market sentiment or mood. The market`s over-all P/E ratio has to be based on the appropriate market index, such as the BSE Sensex or the NSE Nifty. Such an index is computed on the basis of the aggregate market value of the companies covered by the index in relation to the aggregate earnings of the companies concerned, i.e.

$$\frac{\text{Aggregate Market Value}}{\text{Aggregate earnings}}$$

2.10 *In such a computation, the loss-making companies have to be excluded from both the numerator and the denominator. This is because the P/E ratio cannot be computed if the EPS is negative.*

2.11 The market`s average P/E ratio can be helpful in judging whether the market in general is over-valued, under-valued or reasonably valued at the particular time. Historical data for the market`s P/E ratio for atleast the recent years can be helpful in judging the prevailing state of the market. There is a serious risk of loss if one buys stocks when the market is too "hot", as indicated by unusually high P/E ratios.

Equity market's volatile character:

2.12 It has been well said that the *stock market is like a pendulum which for ever goes on swinging between unsustainable optimism and unjustified pessimism.* ***An investor in equity shares should be prepared for such gyrations, both financially and psychologically.***

2.13 Stock prices often behave irrationally: there have been periods of irrational exuberance and also periods of too much gloom. For this reason, the stock market is a volatile place. As an investor one should be prepared for the risk involved in equity investment, taking into account one`s own circumstances, such as the financial position, age, family responsibilities, etc.

2.14 The market`s *average* P/E ratio shows wide movements indicating the market`s volatile character. For example, the P/E ratio for the BSE Sensex and NSE Nifty companies fell sharply to less than one-half within a year and then regained substantially over the next year, and subsequently hovered around this figure as indicated in Table 2.2. Such ups and downs are indicative of the riskiness of investment in shares.

Table 2.2

THE BEHAVIOUR OF P/E RATIO IN RECENT YEARS [2]

Date	*NSE P/E Ratio*	*BSE P/E Ratio*
01.01.08	27.64	27.67
01.01.09	13.3	12.67
31.12.09	23.17	22.36
08.10.10	24.08	25.44

2.15 **Industry-wise P/E ratio:** Some industries are characterised by sharp cyclical behaviour. For example, industries producing capital goods are generally cyclical. Their share price behaviour is also cyclical. In good periods, when their order books are full, their share prices are also booming. In dull periods, their share prices are also down. On the other hand, industries engaged in producing widely used consumer goods usually have a relatively stable behaviour.

Earnings yield:

2.16 Algebraically, earnings yield is the inverse of the P/E ratio. The numerator for computing the earnings yield is the EPS and the denominator is the share price. The earnings yield is computed for individual companies as a percentage, as indicated below:

2. For historial behaviour of share prices in India, see chapter 5.

$$\frac{\text{Earning per share}}{\text{Share price}} \times 100$$

Normally speaking, the higher the earnings yield of a share, the more attractive will be the share as an investment, assuming that other things (such as riskiness and growth prospects) are the same.

Dividend yield:

2.17 Dividend yield is the dividend-per-share for the latest 12 months as percentage of the ruling share price, as indicated below:

$$\frac{\text{Dividend per share}}{\text{Share price}} \times 100$$

Dividend vis-à-vis capital appreciation:

2.18 *The bulk of the return to the investor in shares nowadays takes the form of capital appreciation rather than dividend yield.* Typically, the dividend yield is a relatively small percentage (around 1.0 - 2.5%) of the prevailing share price. The capital appreciation varies with change in share price and is therefore irregular but accounts for the bulk of the return on shares over relatively long-periods. Dividends paid by companies are relatively stable because company managements try to follow a long-term dividend policy, keeping in view the long run prospects of the business.

2.19 Most companies plough back a substantial part of their earnings for financing business expansion internally. On the average, companies in India plough back around

60 - 75% of their earnings. This leads to increased earnings and dividends in the future.

Bonus shares:

2.20 These are shares issued by companies, not for a price but out of accumulated reserves, thereby transforming the reserves into share capital. This process is known as capitalization of reserves. For example, a company may give one bonus share against each existing share, i.e. 1:1, thereby doubling the number of shares. This by itself will not increase the aggregate market value of the company. If the aggregate market value remains the same as before after a bonus issue of, say, 1:1, it would simply be like changing a 10-rupee note into two 5-rupee notes.

2.21. However, the issue of bonus shares is usually regarded very favourably by shareholders. They hope that the company`s management is expecting an increase in profits which may lead to increase in dividend.

Book value per share:

2.22 The book value of a share is its value as per books of account. It is computed as follows: First compute the total *net worth* (i.e., total assets *minus* the liabilities to all outsiders i.e., other than shareholders). Next, divide the total net worth by the number of shares. The resultant is the book value per share. However, such book value can be highly artificial, specially because the present *realisable value* of many assets, such as land, buildings and plant, cannot always be ascertained. Only the current assets, such as cash and bank balance, receivables and inventories of saleable goods, etc., can be fairly accurately valued.

Beta: Meaning and significance:

2.23 The term "beta" indicates the sensitivity (volatility) of an individual stock`s price to changes in the level of the market index. The market index measures the general market movements.

2.24 Some individual stocks may rise *and* fall realtivley *faster than the general market* (i.e. market index). These are high beta stocks. They are more volatile than the market as a whole.

2.25 If a stock`s price changes (i.e. rises or falls) *by the same percentage as the market index*, it will be said to have a beta of 1. Thus, if the market index rises (or falls) by 10%, and the particular stock also rises (or falls) by 10%, it will be said to have a beta of 1. That is, it is just as volatile as the market as a whole.

2.26 On the other hand, if a stock`s price fluctuates twice as much as the market index, such a stock will be said to have a beta of 2. It will be regarded as highly risky. High beta stocks can be very rewarding during a bull market but very disappointing during a bear market. An investor needs to be very cautious while dealing with high-beta stocks.

2.27 Further, if a stock has low beta of, say, 0.5, it indicates that it fluctuates (rises or falls) to the extent of only one-half compared to the market index. Its price will be relatively stable and it is, therefore, less risky than the market as a whole as represented by the market index. At the same time, it also means that low beta stocks are laggards during a bull run as they would fall behind the general market. Thus, low beta stocks lose their charm in a bull market but they provide much solace during bear market phase.

2.28 *Whether a stock has high beta or low beta is, to a large extent, related to the nature of the underlying industry.* For example, shares of companies catering to mass consumption would generally have relatively low beta. On the other hand, shares of companies engaged in sectors like capital goods, real estate comprising land and buildings, etc., would generally have relatively high beta.

2.29 The concept of beta can help investors in choosing the basket of stocks according to the characteristics which suit their temperament and circumstances.

3

Choosing the Right Companies for Investing

Importance of choosing the right companies:

3.1 From the investor's viewpoint, choosing the right companies for investing in their shares is very crucial for attaining good return over the long-term. This is understandable. It requires a strategy of choosing a relatively small number of outstanding companies and investing the bulk of the investible funds in their shares for the long-term.[1] In this way, the investor would have a very good chance of earning a good return over the long term, ignoring the day-to-day ups and downs. The

1. See Robert G. Hagstrom, *The Warren Buffett Portfolio*, p.1

daily ups and downs of the market are of no consequence for the long-term investor.

How to choose the right companies:

3.2 Selecting the right companies requires consideration of two distinct aspects, viz., (a) the nature of the underlying business and (b) the quality of management. Each of these two aspects are explained below in detail.

THE NATURE OF BUSINESS

3.3 As regards the nature of the underlying business, the investor needs to evaluate the company's economic fundamentals. In this regard, three characteristics demand special attention, viz., (a) prospects of business growth (b) nature of risks and (c) competitive strength. These are explained below:

(a) Growth prospects:

The investor should choose companies which have the capability to achieve a relatively high rate of growth in sales (i.e. top-line growth) as well as growth in net profit (i.e., bottom-line growth).[2] This will depend on whether the companies chosen have products or services with good market potential for many years. A related point in this context is that the growth potential of existing

---

2. Sales are shown in the top-line and the profit is shown in the bottom line of the Income Statement. Hence the terms "top-line growth" and "bottom-line growth". Top-line growth (i.e. sales growth) is important as the real source of profit growth (i.e. bottom-line growth).

products is likely to get exhausted over a period due to saturation of the market and the emergence of competitors. Long-term continuance of growth will depend on continuous innovation through Research and Development. How much emphasis a management places on Research and Development is therefore important. The future rate of return to the shareholders will be affected also by how the growth is financed, i.e. whether by ploughing back earnings, or by issuing new shares or by borrowing.

(b) **Competitive strength:**

The companies chosen should possess competitive strength which is necessary for ensuring their long-term survival as well as growth. A company may have a strong leading position because of its brand or reputation for quality. The other companies may not be so reputed. During boom time, all companies may have their order books full. However, when a slow down occurs, the less reputed companies will be the most affected and some of them may not even survive if the slow down lasts long.

(c) **Nature of risks:**

Some businesses are cyclical in nature, such as those engaged in manufacture of capital goods, like machinery, steel, cement, etc. The length of such cycles varies from industry to industry. The profits earned by these businesses are also characterized by cyclical fluctuations. So are the share prices of such companies. On the other hand, industries engaged in the production and supply of goods or services for mass consumption are generally not cyclical in nature.

3.4 Companies in cyclical businesses should have the financial and management capacity to survive through a prolonged deep depression. For example, too much dependence on debt financing can threaten a company`s existence because interest on borrowed money must be paid even though the company is suffering a loss.

QUALITY OF MANAGEMENT

Attributes of good management:

3.5 Apart from the general managerial quality, what matters most from the investor's viewpoint is the management's integrity and honesty as well as real concern for the shareholders and even the general public. The companies having such management enjoy great respect of the general public. It indirectly benefits the companies concerned.

3.6 The management's quality may be evaluated specially in terms of the following attributes:

- Integrity and honesty: The integrity must be unquestionable. Many managements are more interested in enriching themselves through dubious means than in enriching the shareholders.
- Entrepreneurial ability: This can be judged from the background of the promoters and their past history.

- Willingness to observe disclosure standards and to respect the outside shareholders' rights: This can be judged from the behaviour of the promoters, specially their frankness to admit mistakes and their readiness to address the shareholders' concerns and queries.
- Readiness to address the concerns of the general public: This will enhance the promoting group`s public image and will indirectly benefit the company.

Dividend distribution policy:

3.7 A policy of constant enhancement of dividend distribution over a long term is indicative both of the company's improving business success and of the management's determination to reward the shareholders. The dedication to shareholder value can be judged to some extent by the company's dividend distribution policy. Of course, a company's management has to decide how much profit to distribute by way of dividend and how much to plough back in the business.

KNOW THE COMPANIES

Limit your share portfolio:

3.8 An investor who limits his investing to companies and businesses which he understands would have a greater chance of doing well. As an investor, one can get some useful clues about a company in relation to its competitors by *gathering information from those who are familiar with the company*, such as some existing or former employees, suppliers of services or materials, and others who may be concerned in one way or another with the company. Such information has to be collected very tactfully without breaching the insider trading regulations.

3.9 To be able to "know" the companies and follow them up, the individual investor should ordinarily limit the share portfolio to a relatively small number of companies, say, around 5 to 12,[3] or nearabout that.

3.10 Instead of increasing the number of companies in his portfolio, the investor may adopt the strategy of buying more shares of the same companies on market dips, thereby lowering his average acquisition cost. This is a good practical strategy.

Extreme caution needed:

3.11 According to Philip Fisher, a highly respected authority, investing in shares is inherently risky and should therefore be only out of funds which are "truly surplus" in the sense that the investor`s family will not be seriously hurt in case of loss.[4] For example, the investor`s children may be too young and yet to complete their education. Thus, an investor`s family circumstances matter a great deal when considering whether and how much to invest

---

3. Peter Lynch has observed that owning stocks is like having children and one should have a limit. He feels that a part-time investor in stocks can at best follow around 8-12 companies. See Peter Lynch with John Rothchild, *Beating the Street* (Simon & Schuster, New York, 1993), p.303.
4. Philip Fisher, *Common Stocks and Uuncommon Profits,* (p.86)

in shares. This implies a very cautions policy as against being reckless towards investing in equities.

3.12 Warren Buffett indirectly makes the same point by suggesting that unless an investor can watch the value of his share holdings decline by as much as 50% *without becoming panic-stricken,* he should not invest in shares.[5]

WHAT ARE 'RIGHT' COMPANIES

Invest within your circle of competence:

3.13 An important point often missed is that **the right companies would not be the same for all individual investors because of differences in their personal backgrounds**. For example, a medical doctor will normally be in a better position to judge stocks of pharmaceutical companies compared to a non-medical investor. Similarly, an individual working in an engineering company or in an information technology company would have advantage of another kind. Thus, each one's advantage in selecting investments could vary.

3.14 Once an investor has bought a stock, he would have learnt something about the industry and the company' place within it. The knowledge and insights thus acquired can be of immense value in deciding where to put more money.

3.15 **It is always better to invest in companies which are within one's "circle of competence", i.e., companies and businesses which one understands.**

5. See Robert Hagstrom, *The Warren Buffett Way*, p.53

4

Investing in Initial Public Offers (IPOs)

Historical Background:

4.1 Before the creation of SEBI as the statutory regulator of the Indian capital market in 1992, there used to be the Controller of Capital Issues in the Union Ministry of Finance. The Controller used to decide which companies were to be allowed to make issues of shares and securities to the public and on what terms. This responsibility was transferred to SEBI in 1992. The SEBI introduced the system of free pricing, allowing companies to decide the issue price, based on some basic guidelines. This encouraged many unlisted companies to come out with IPOs. Some of the IPOs were good but there were quite a few cases of fly-by-night entrepreneurs to jump into the fray and vanish after collecting money from the public.[1]

IPOs vis-à-vis buying existing shares:

4.2 An investor interested in shares may choose to buy existing shares from the secondary market or may choose to invest in IPOs, i.e. initial public offers by unlisted companies wanting to expand their business.

4.3 Purchases from the secondary market usually offer no bargains. On the other hand, some IPOs may provide opportunity for quick and substantial profits depending on the public response. Applicants for IPOs are ranked on the basis of book building, i.e., applicants offering to buy the shares at a higher price are given preference while allotting the shares.

4.4 The post-listing price in the case of some IPOs may be higher than the cut-off price because of heavy subscription and also because of quotas for specific categories, such as retail investors, high networth individuals, etc.

Relationship of new issue market to secondary market:

4.5 There is a close relationship between the new issue market and the secondary market for the existing listed shares. When the secondary market is booming, the new issues tend to rise. This is because some investors may feel that the market prices of existing shares are too high and, therefore, they turn their attention to purchase of suitable new issues.

---

1. Between 1992 and 2001, as many as 238 companies had vanished after raising capital. Only 117 of these companies could be traced by a team comprising representatives of the Ministry of Corporate Affairs and SEBI. However, no action against the promoters of the companies concerned seems to have been taken.

Empirical data:

4.6 An all-India survey of household investors conducted around mid-2007, posed a question whether buying IPOs is better than buying existing shares or is it the other way round? Interestingly, the answers indicated that IPOs have an edge over purchases made from the secondary market.[2] The results of the survey are summarized below:

		Percentage of respondents
(a)	Buying IPOs is better	43.68
(b)	Buying existing shares is better	30.08
	(a) + (b) =	73.76
(c)	Undecided	26.24
	Total	100.00

Note: The number of households covered across the country was 1463.

Chart 4.1 highlights the results in visual form.

Chart 4.1: IPOs vis-a-vis Buying Existing Shares

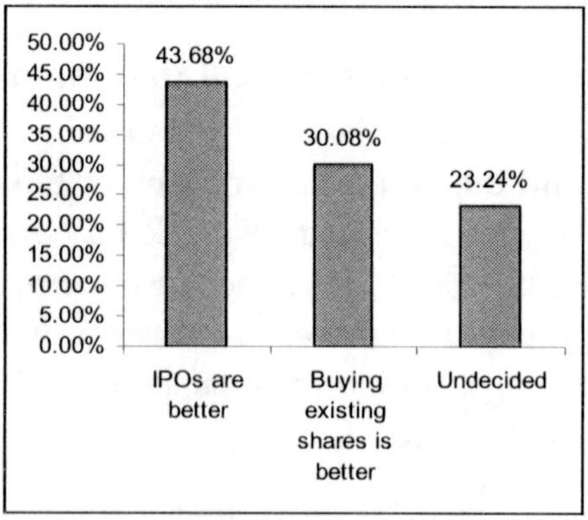

2. This is based on the report entitled *The Changing Investment Preferences of Indian Households*, directed by L.C. Gupta and Naveen Jain on behalf of the Society for Capital Market Research & Development, published in 2008.

4.7 Slightly more than one-fourth (26.24% to be exact) of the respondents were undecided. However, the balance of advantage is clearly in favour of IPOs. That is why the IPO market attracts quite a large number of applicants.

4.8 The volume of IPOs during the last six years has varied from year to year as shown in Table 4.1. The returns from investing in IPOs have also varied considerably among the IPOs floated in different years, depending on the prevailing market conditions. Apart from the general market conditions, there are also sector-specific factors, such as the realty sector sometimes attracting great attention and at other times being out of favour. Thus, the timing as well as the sector can make a tremendous difference.

Table 4.1 : VOLUME OF IPOs IN INDIA

2004-05		2005-06		2006-07		2007-08		2008-09		2009-10	
No.	Amount (Rs. crore)	No.	Amount (Rs. crore)	No.	Amount (Rs. crore)	No.	Amount (Rs. crore)	No.	Amount (Rs. crore)	No.	Amount (Rs. crore)
23	12,382	79	10,936	77	28,504	85	42,595	21	2,082	39	24,696

Source: SEBI Bulletins for various years.

Bewildering variety of IPOs:

4.9 IPOs range over a bewildering variety in terms of their quality and background. On the one hand are highly successful and reputed family-owned businesses, like Godrej, Nirma, etc., being sold as going concerns to the public. At the other extreme are unknown enterprises with indifferent performance or short, unreliable histories, coming out with a public offer in order to expand their scale of operations or add new lines of business.

Quotas for investor categories:

4.10 As part of regulation of the IPO market, SEBI has prescribed quotas for certain categories of investors, such as retail investors, Qualified Institutional Buyers (QIBs) and High Networth Individuals. The QIBs are long-term investors and their presence is likely to ensure rigorous scrutiny of the issues. Most of the retail investors are not capable of carrying out such scrutiny. Presence of QIBs as firm allottees ensures a sound and economical system of issuing securities without interfering with the free market principle.

4.11 The IPO process has been speeded up considerably. Such process from the receipt of applications upto the finalization of allotments and refunds used to take months. Hence, the money paid by applicants remained blocked for considerable time, resulting in interest loss for the applicants. The whole process has been revised considerably to prevent such loss. The SEBI has introduced a system under which the application money remains in the applicant`s bank account till the allotment process is completed. (This is the system of ASBA, i.e., Applications Supported by Blocked Amount).

Key role of the promoters:

4.12 The general reputation of promoters of a company counts a lot in regard to the public response to an IPO. Many established promoters already have several companies under their control and enjoy high reputation among investors. There are also less known promoters who do not enjoy much reputation and have to make extra effort to attract investors. A substantial part of the funding is brought or arranged by the promoters.

Angel investors:

4.13 In some cases, there are the so-called *angel investors* who may be family friends or close acquaintances of the promoters and are prepared to invest in the project. They are interested in promising start-ups.

Private Equity Firms:

4.14 There are also *private equity* firms which, if they are satisfied with the business proposition, may agree to join hands with the promoters at the early stage of an enterprise.

Venture capitalists:

4.15 Another category comprises *venture capitalists.* They closely examine the prospects of the business and soundness of the project. If they are convinced, they may take a stake in the project. They are not permanent investors. Actually, the line between venture capital and private equity is rather thin. Both these categories would like to dispose of the investment at an appropriate time. They go on exploring other opportunities for investing as venture capitalists or private equity firms, thus rotating their money.

Grading of IPOs:

4.16 The ordinary investor has serious difficulty in evaluating the soundness of an IPO. It was in recognition of this problem that SEBI decided to introduce a grading system for IPOs on mandatory basis. This came into effect from May 1, 2007.

4.17 SEBI had first experimented with grading of IPOs on voluntary basis. It framed guidelines for grading but these were purely recommendatory in nature. As per the Guidelines, the issuers were required to state on the cover of the offer document whether they have opted for grading. In that case, the grade was to be disclosed in the prospectus.[3] However, none of the promoters and lead managers voluntarily chose to be graded even at no cost to the companies concerned. This is what led SEBI to make grading of all IPOs compulsory but the grading exercise, as per SEBI`s explicit decision, was not to cover the issue price. The SEBI has required that all IPOs be compulsorily graded. It was thought that such grading would help to improve the general quality of IPOs.

The grades:

4.18 Grading is done on a 5-Point scale. The highest grade is 5/5, followed by 4/5, 3/5, 2/5 and 1/5. The highest grade 5/5 indicates strong fundamentals, 4/5 indicates above average fundamentals; 3/5 average fundamentals, 2/5 below average fundamentals; and 1/5 poor fundamentals.

4.19 A visual representation of the grades from the highest (5/5) to the lowest (1/5) is presented in Chart 4. 2.

---

3. See Annual Report of SEBI for 2006-07, p.11.

Chart 4.2

VISUAL PRESENTATION OF GRADES

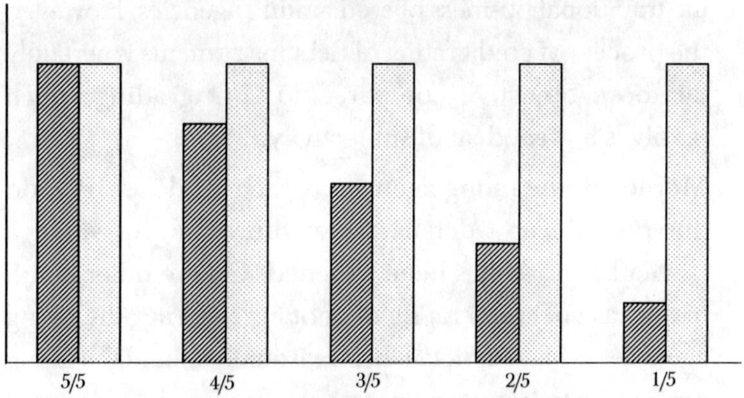

Grading is done by credit rating agencies:

4.20 There was also the question as to who should be given the responsibility for grading. Should it be merchant bankers who whet and manage new issues or somebody else? As per SEBI's decision, the grading of IPOs is done by one of the recognised credit rating agencies. It was a good practical decision.

4.21 Of course, credit rating is concerned with debt instruments and assesses the risk of defaults on the part of the debtor. It is a long established practice. On the other hand, grading of Initial Public Offers (IPOs) is a very different cup of tea and an altogether new idea, requiring a different approach.

Shortcomings of IPO grading system:

4.22 The issuing company chooses the rating agency for grading its IPO. The issuing company also pays the expenses. There is an inherent *conflict of interest* in this arrangement. Of course, such conflict of interests exists even in the rating of debt instruments which constitute the traditional business of credit-rating agencies. However, the process of credit rating of debt instruments is certainly far more objective compared to IPO grading which involves a great deal of subjectivity.

4.23. Moreover, the rating agencies, which grade an IPO, do not provide any details about the basis on which a particular grade has been assigned. On the other hand, in the case of credit rating of debt instruments, the rating agencies explain in detail their reasoning behind the rating assigned, such as weaknesses, strengths, the nature of risks, etc.

4.24 It may also be noted that *only 5 grades have been prescribed by SEBI,* respectively indicating (a) strong fundamentals, (b) above average fundamentals, (c) average fundamentals, (d) below average fundamentals, and (e) poor fundamentals, as mentioned earlier. However, in the case debt instruments the rating agencies provide finer and far more detailed categories plus detailed explanations and reasons. The topmost rating, indicating highest safety in the case of debt instruments is AAA (pronounced as Triple A). The rating hierarchy for debt instruments is long, making subtle differences. For example, the rating agency ICRA`s scale has 8 categories, as illustrated below from top to bottom:

AAA

AA

A

BBB

BB

B

C (substantial risk)

D (already in default)

The reality of IPO performance:

4.25 Really speaking, the future performance of a company coming out with an IPO is difficult to forecast. An analysis was made by *The Economic Times*, dated 29th September 2009, covering 277 IPOs which got listed in January 2006. While nearly two-thirds showed gains immediately after listing, the proportion of companies staying above their issue price declined rapidly. Three years since the listing, only 31% of the issues could maintain their prices above their respective issue prices. This means that there is 69% probability that a share will trade below the offer price by the end of the third year after listing.

Need for caution:

4.26. The merchant bankers along with promoters do their best to price the issue aggressively. As a result, there is not much left on the table for the ordinary investors. This amounts in some cases to almost looting the ordinary investors. Hence, investors need to be specially cautions while investing in IPOs.

4.27 It was hoped that grading of IPOs in terms of their fundamental quality would enable investors to steer clear of unsound IPOs because these are likely to be restrained by the grading system as, in all probability, they will be in the bottom grades of 1 and 2. There is as yet no empirical evidence to show that the future performance of the various IPOs is related to the grade assigned to each.

4.28 **In any case, the most serious shortcoming of the grading system is that it does not cover the issue price which is often hyped, as we have mentioned above.** The grading system does not indicate whether and how far the issue price can be regarded as fair and reasonable. **From the investor`s viewpoint, the issue price is a most critical factor in determining the worthwhileness of investing in an IPO. For example, if the issue is priced beyond a certain level, it may not at all be worthwhile investing. An over-priced issue is most likely to result in loss for the investors.**

Too much subjectivity:

4.29 The grading exercise is supposed to take into account the fundamental factors which determine the soundness of an IPO, such as the competitive strength of the company as well as the competence and integrity of the company`s management. The regulations about grading are silent about what factors ought to be taken into account for grading. This has been completely left to the grading agencies. A great deal of subjectivity is thus involved.

Credit rating versus IPO grading:

4.30 Unlike the credit rating system which is well established and widely relied upon by lenders for judging the safety of the funds lent, the utility of the IPO grading system has been somewhat controversial. No empirical evidence is presently available to show whether the post-issue gain on various IPOs is closely related to the grades assigned, i.e. whether such gain is consistently and distinctly higher for issues which were assigned higher grades. The grading system cannot yet to regarded as a dependable guide for the investing public for choosing the more promising IPOs.

Concluding comments:

4.31 **Perhaps, much more than the grading system, it is the willingness to invest in the IPOs by knowledgeable entities, like Qualified Institutional Buyers, private equity firms and venture capitalists which can make a real difference to the quality of the IPO market.**

5

The Share Price Behaviour

Need for a historical perspective:

5.1 For understanding the likely behaviour of share prices in the future, one needs to look at how stocks have actually behaved in the past over sufficiently long periods and under varying conditions. An investor who has acquired a good understanding of share price behaviour can be expected to invest more intelligently and also more cautiously. He is less likely to be surprised and shocked. At the same time, he would be better prepared mentally and financially for the risks and rewards involved.

Actual behaviour of Indian equity prices:

5.2 Chart 5.1 depicts the behaviour of equity prices in India over the period 1980-2010 based on the BSE Sensex.

The Sensex is based on 30 leading companies. It provides the longest series of equity prices in India covering 30 years, starting from 1980 till date.

5.3 There is another index of Indian equity prices called Nifty, which covers 50 companies, and is compiled by the National Stock Exchange. It has a much shorter history, as it is available from 1996 only (see Chart 5.2). The BSE Sensex and the NSE Nifty move largely in a parallel manner because many of the companies are included in both.

Equity prices over the long-term:

5.4 Over the long-term (say, 10-15 years), equity prices tend to rise. This is mainly because most companies distribute just a minor proportion (around 25-40%) of their earnings and plough back the rest, leading to rise in earnings per share (EPS). Another reason for long term rise in equity prices is the general inflationary tendency. Investment in equities is regarded as a kind of hedge against inflation, attracting many long-term savers. The long-term behaviour of Sensex is depicted in Chart 5.1. The highest level it touched was 21,207 (see Table 5.3). However it fell sharply over the next nine months. The average annual rise in Sensex over its 30 years of existence upto the highest peak touched by it implies a return 19-20% per annum, as indicated by Table 5.1, ignoring the ups and downs from time to time. (Table 5.1 indicates the growth of an initial sum of Rs. 100 over the different lengths of time at various assumed rates of return.)

---

1. See *Indian Securities Market: A Review*, Volume XII 2009, published by the National Stock Exchange of India, p.15.

Chart 5.1

BSE SENSEX FROM JANUARY 1980 TO SEPTEMBER 2010
(LAST DAY'S CLOSING VALUE OF EVERY MONTH)

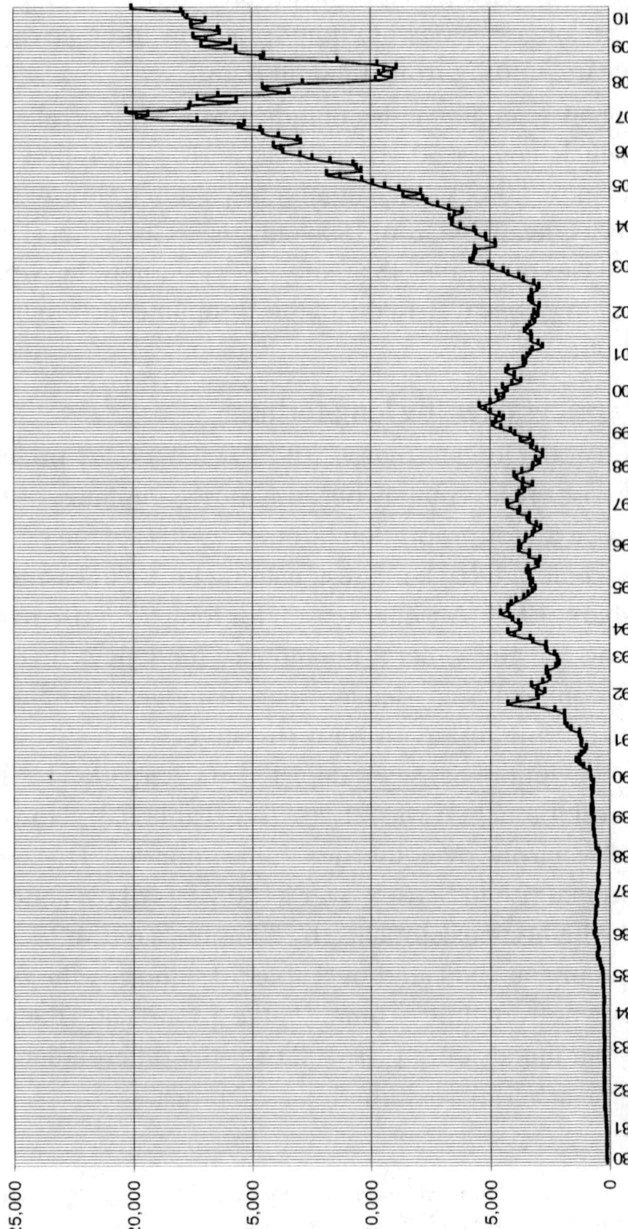

Chart 5.2
NSE NIFTY FROM JANUARY 1996 TO SEPTEMBER 2010
[LAST DAY'S CLOSING VALUE OF EVERY MONTH]

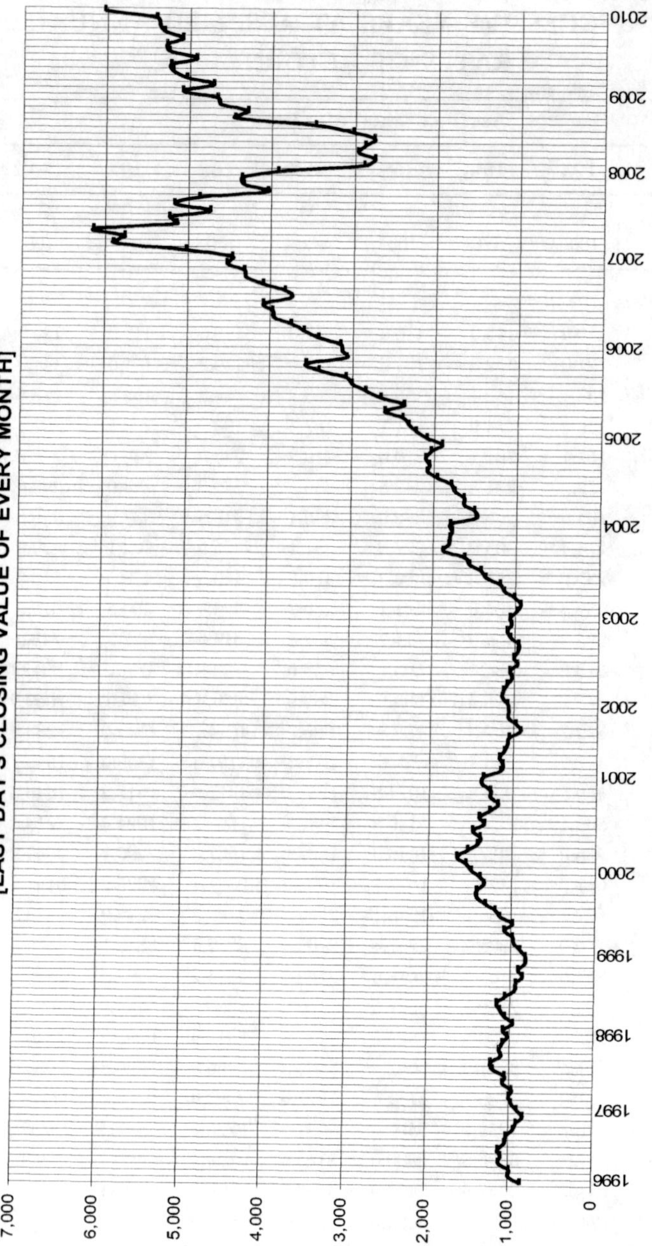

Table 5.1 : GROWTH OF INITIAL SUM OF Rs. 100 OVER SUCCESSIVE YEARS AT ASSUMED ANNUAL RATES OF RETURN

	Assumed rate of return							
	5%	10%	15%	16%	17%	18%	19%	20%
Initial Sum	100	100	100	100	100	100	100	100
Years								
1	105.0	110.0	115.0	116.0	117.0	118.0	119.0	120.0
2	110.3	121.0	132.3	134.6	136.9	139.2	141.6	144.0
3	115.8	133.1	152.1	156.1	160.2	164.3	168.5	172.8
4	121.6	146.4	174.9	181.1	187.4	193.9	200.5	207.4
5	127.6	161.1	201.1	210.0	219.2	228.8	238.6	248.8
6	134.0	177.2	231.3	243.6	256.5	270.0	284.0	298.6
7	140.7	194.9	266.0	282.6	300.1	318.5	337.9	358.3
8	147.7	214.4	305.9	327.8	351.1	375.9	402.1	430.0
9	155.1	235.8	351.8	380.3	410.8	443.5	478.5	516.0
10	162.9	259.4	404.6	441.1	480.7	523.4	569.5	619.2
11	171.0	285.3	465.2	511.7	562.4	617.6	677.7	743.0
12	179.6	313.8	535.0	593.6	658.0	728.8	806.4	891.6
13	188.6	345.2	615.3	688.6	769.9	859.9	959.6	1069.9
14	198.0	379.7	707.6	798.8	900.7	1014.7	1142.0	1283.9
15	207.9	417.7	813.7	926.6	1053.9	1197.4	1359.0	1540.7
16	218.3	459.5	935.8	1074.8	1233.0	1412.9	1617.2	1848.8
17	229.2	505.4	1076.1	1246.8	1442.6	1667.2	1924.4	2218.6
18	240.7	556.0	1237.5	1446.3	1687.9	1967.3	2290.1	2662.3
19	252.7	611.6	1423.2	1677.7	1974.8	2321.4	2725.2	3194.8
20	265.3	672.7	1636.7	1946.1	2310.6	2739.3	3242.9	3833.8
21	278.6	740.0	1882.2	2257.4	2703.4	3232.4	3859.1	4600.5
22	292.5	814.0	2164.5	2618.6	3162.9	3814.2	4592.3	5520.6
23	307.2	895.4	2489.1	3037.6	3700.6	4500.8	5464.9	6624.7
24	322.5	985.0	2862.5	3523.6	4329.7	5310.9	6503.2	7949.7
25	338.6	1083.5	3291.9	4087.4	5065.8	6266.9	7738.8	9539.6
26	355.6	1191.8	3785.7	4741.4	5927.0	7394.9	9209.2	11447.5
27	373.3	1311.0	4353.5	5500.0	6934.5	8726.0	10958.9	13737.1
28	392.0	1442.1	5006.6	6380.0	8113.4	10296.7	13041.1	16484.5
29	411.6	1586.3	5757.5	7400.9	9492.7	12150.1	15518.9	19781.4
30	432.2	1744.9	6621.2	8585.0	11106.5	14337.1	18467.5	23737.6

Short-term price behaviour:

5.5 Over the short-term, the equity prices usually behave in a zigzag manner showing sharp swings due to many factors, both economic and political. Further, both domestic and external events have a bearing on the behaviour of the domestic equity prices. For example, in the case of India, the flow of foreign funds into Indian equity market has been an important influence.

5.6 *The magnitude of ups and downs in equity prices is considerable. For example, the Sensex fell from around 21000 level in early 2008 to well below 10,000 within a year. The percentage fall in the Nifty was of a similar magnitude.* **As an equity investor, one should be prepared mentally and financially for sharp short-term swings in equity prices. For this reason, it would be advisable for ordinary investors to limit the percentage of wealth held in the form of equity shares.**

5.7 The percentage should ordinarily be lower for those nearing retirement than for the younger people who can afford to have a much longer time-horizon than older people. The younger people have a better chance to recoup the decline in share values as they can take a long view.

Dividend vs. capital appreciation:

5.8 The return earned by shareholders is partly in the form of cash dividend and partly by way of rise in the share price. The dividend component of the total return has declined significantly since around 1980. For the companies comprising the Sensex, the average dividend yield used to be as high as approximately 5.1% of the prevailing share prices during 1980-85.[2] The average yield for this group of companies has gradually come down very considerably. The dividend yield varies among individual companies. It should be remembered that dividend yield refers to the year`s dividend per share as per cent of the prevailing market price. The dividend yields are now mostly between 1.0% and 2.5% in the case of leading shares.

5.9 *It needs to be understood that this is not because of decline in dividend per share. Actually, dividend per share has been increasing in the case of successful and well-managed companies but share values have been rising faster. Thus, capital appreciation has become the more important part of the total return on equity shares.*

Be prepared for wild swings:

5.10 Historical observation of equity prices shows wild movements over relatively short periods. For example, consider the one-year period from April 7, 2009 to April 6, 2010. This period saw sharp movements in the equity prices: the Sensex rose to the height of 18,048 on 7.4.2009 and then fell to 11,621 on 11.05.2009, representing a fall of 35.6% over this very short period (see Table 5.2). The Nifty showed a similar magnitude of fall over the same period.

5.11 Now, consider a medium period of 3 years from 7.05.2007 to 6.05.2010 and look at the movements of the Sensex within this period (see Table 5.3). It was

2. See L.C. Gupta and Utpal Choudhury, *Returns on Indian Equity Shares* (published by the Society for Capital Market Research & Development, 2000), p.30. For historical data, see L.C. Gupta *Rates of Return on Equities: The Indian Experience* (Oxford Universtiy Press, Delhi. 1981).

during this period that the Sensex touched 21,207 as on 10.01.2008. This is the highest level ever reached by Sensex in its entire history. Subsequently, it declined to 7697 by 27.10.2008, i.e. a fall of 63.7% from the peak within about 9 months. The Nifty showed a similar movement. The Sensex and the Nifty often show parallel movements because many of the stocks are common to both.

5.12 The important point is the unpredictability of equity prices over relatively short periods. An investor in equities should be prepared mentally and financially for quite wild swings. This is in the very nature of the market for equities.

Table 5.2

EQUITY PRICES MOVEMENT OVER 1 YEAR

Sensex			*Nifty*		
High (as on 7.04.2009)	*Low (as on* 1.05.2009)	*% fall*	*High (as on* 07.04.2009)	*Low (as on* 07.05.2009)	*% fall*
18047.86	11621.30	35.61	5399.65	3534.20	34.55

Table 5.3

EQUITY PRICES MOVEMENT OVER 3 YEARS

Sensex			*Nifty*		
High (as on 10.01.2008)	*Low (as on* 7.10.2008)	*% fall*	*High (as on* 8.01.2008)	*Low (as on* 27.10.2008)	*% fall*
21206.77	7697.39	63.70	6357.10	2252.75	64.56

6

Share Buybacks by Companies

Relatively new practice in India:

6.1. Investors need to understand the system of share buyback. This is a relatively new practice in India. It was introduced in India in October 1998.

6.2 It may be mentioned in passing that the U.S. was the first country to have the practice of share buybacks as early as the 1970s. Thus, the idea of share buyback originated in the U.S. and later on spread to other countries. The U.S. companies can be regarded as having innovated this corporate practice.

The basic idea:

6.3 Share buyback refers to a listed company buying its own shares from the existing shareholders upto a defined quantity within a defined price limit. A company is not allowed to buyback its shares so as to delist the shares from the stock exchange. The central idea behind share buyback is to boost the return on equity by using surplus cash which is truly surplus in the sense that it is not required by the company in the foreseeable future.

What led the Indian government to allow share buyback?

6.4 The immediate reason which prompted the Indian government around 1996 to consider the introduction of the share buyback system was the prolonged depression in the stock market. Share buyback system was expected to remedy this problem. The Government of India decided to implement the share buyback system on urgent basis through an Ordinance promulgated on 31st October 1998. Later on, the Companies (Amendment) Act 1999 was enacted and was deemed to have come into force from the date of the Ordinance.

How share buybacks can help:

6.5 There are several reasons why a company may decide to buyback its own shares. These are briefly indicated below:

(a) Firstly, as already mentioned above, the company has surplus cash which is not required by it in the foreseeable future. If such surplus cash is returned to the shareholders, it would benefit the company as well as its shareholders. It will also be good for the economy in general by promoting better use of the country's capital resources. Continuing to hold surplus cash pulls down the rate of return earned by the company on the total assets. This would ultimately affect the shareholder value adversely. Share buyback would enable the shareholders to invest this money in a more profitable way.[1]

(b) Of course, surplus cash, if represented by profits earned, can also be returned to shareholders by distributing a higher dividend. However, this would mean highly fluctuating dividends, creating uncertainty in the minds of investors. Hence well-managed companies attempt to pay steady and rising dividend rather than fluctuating dividends.

(c) Further, a company can enhance the earnings per share through buyback of shares. A company`s total earnings can be expected to be maintained if the share buyback is out of surplus cash, which is truly surplus. Moreover, share buyback will reduce the total number of shares, thereby increasing the per share earnings.

(d) Still another argument in favour of share buyback system is that the shares of many small and medium-sized companies are not tradable or they can be traded only at heavy discounts. Share buyback system can provide a better exit route to shareholders in such cases as it would enable them to realize a better price.

---

1. See *The Economist* leader entitled "Share Non-sense", August 15, 1998, pp. 13-14.

(e) Share buybacks can be helpful in conveying to investors that the market is currently undervaluing the company`s shares and that the proposed share buyback would facilitate recognition of the true value of the shares.

The promoters' viewpoint:

6.6 From the promoters` point of view, share buybacks enable the promoters to increase their *relative* voting power without having to invest their own money. Share buyback is out of the company`s funds. Legally, the promoters are not prohibited from offering their shares for buyback but they usually do not offer their shares for buyback by the company. If promoters intend to offer their shares for buyback by the company, this has to be disclosed.

Empirical findings on effect of share buyback:

6.7 Empirical data supports the generally favourable effects of share buybacks from the shareholders` viewpoint. A comparison of a sample of companies which had resorted to share buyback with non-buyback companies had shown that a significantly greater proportion of buyback companies had increased their EPS after the buyback compared to non-buyback companies.[2]

6.8 A company`s dividend per share is usually expected to increase after the company buys back some of its shares.

---

2. See L.C. Gupta, Naveen Jain and Anil Kumar, *Indian Share Buyback Practices & Their Regulation* (Published by the Society for Capital Market Research & Development, 2006, specially tables 5.4 and 5.5, pp. 84 and 86.

This is because the total number of shares is reduced after buyback but the profits available for distribution are unlikely to be affected by share buyback. In fact, it has been found that the EPS in most cases increases due to share buyback. Some step up in dividend may be expected when a company`s EPS has gone up. Of course, changes in dividend are a matter of deliberate policy and are usually made with a time lag.

6.9 Share buyback can be regarded as a minor kind of financial engineering which generally has a favourable effect in the immediate future on the share price, the EPS and the dividend. This finding is supported by the theory behind share buyback. Of course, the fortunes of a company are affected by a great variety of factors, specially over long periods.

Methods of Share Buyback:

6.10 A share buyback offer may be either (a) *Tender Offer* or (b) *Open Market Offer.*

6.11 **Tender offers:** In the case of tender offer, the company commits itself to buyback a definite number of shares from the existing holders on a proportionate basis. Tender Offers may be fixed-price buyback offers or they may be auction-based offers, using a *reverse* book-building procedure. In the normal book-building procedure used for allotting new issues, the book-building starts from the *highest bidders* and stops at the cut-off point at which the shares to be allotted are all exhausted. On the other hand, the reverse book-building starts with the *lowest bidders* and stops when the quota of shares to be bought back is exhausted. This minimises the buy-back cost. It may be mentioned in passing that the regulations prohibit share buyback from any person through negotiated deals.

6.12 **Open market offers:** Under the share buyback regulations in India, a company going for open market method has to announce the "maximum price" limit for repurchase of its shares without committing to buy any definite number of shares at any price within the price limit. Hence, at what price, on which days and in what quantity the company will repurchase its shares are all at the discretion of the company`s management. How the discretion will be exercised and the considerations guiding the management are, in practice, not disclosed to the public.

More transparency needed:

6.13 It may be noted in this context that in the case of open market offers in India, there is no transparency in the buyback procedure. In several instances of open market offers, the companies did not buyback a single share even though the market price of the shares had fallen much below the *maximum authorized price* for the buyback. In certain cases, the authorized amount for buyback was too low.

6.14 Disclosure of only the *maximum authorized price* is of no use to shareholders. What is required from shareholders` point of view is disclosure of the *minimum support price.*

7

Corporate Governance of Listed Companies: The Investor's Angle

Growing importance:

7.1 The quality of corporate governance is of great importance to the shareholders. It is also important for the society in general because large corporations in particular affect the lives of millions of people, the distribution of wealth and incomes, as also the economy's growth. Hence, the Board of Directors of such corporations carries great responsibility. It is a kind of trusteeship responsibility towards the society as a whole. Clause 49 of the Listing Agreement lays down the requirements to be fulfilled by listed companies in India regarding corporate governance. The subject has continued to attract much public attention in India because of some glaring cases of corporate misgovernance.

Historical background:

7.2 In India the first official committee on corporate governance was the Kumar Mangalam Birla Committee constituted by SEBI in May 1999. The committee particularly emphasized the role of the *Independent Directors* for ensuring proper corporate governance. It also suggested the setting up of independent audit committee by the company's Board of Directors in order to enhance the credibility of financial disclosures. Thereafter two other committees, viz. the Naresh Chandra Committee and the Narayan Murthy Committee made further recommendations for strengthening the corporate governance system in India.

U.K.'s Cadbury Committee:

7.3 We may note here that the original impetus towards improving the system of corporate governance was provided by the report of the U.K.'s Cadbury Committee, entitled *The Financial Aspects of Corporate Governance.*[1] The Cadbury Committee defined the essence of corporate governance in the following words:

"Corporate governance is the system by which companies are directed and controlled. Boards of directors are responsible for the governance of their companies. The shareholders' role in governance is to

1. The committee was set up in the U.K. in May 1991 by the London Stock Exchange Financial Reporting Council. Its chairman was sir Adrian Cadbury. Its report was published in 1992.

appoint the directors and auditors and to satisfy themselves that an appropriate governance structure is in place. The responsibilities of the board include setting the company's strategic aim, providing leadership to put them into effect, supervising the management of the business and reporting to shareholders on their stewardship".[2]

Consequences of Enron debacle of 2001:

7.4 The U.S. passed the Sarbanes-Oxley Act in 2002 which greatly tightened the responsibilities of the auditor and made both the company's Chief Executive and the Chief Financial Officer responsible for the accuracy of the financial statements. These events in the U.S. had their echo in India also.

Need for clarity:

7.5 There has also been successive reforms in the system of corporate governance and considerable effort to bring clarity about what the board of directors is supposed to do, how the board should be composed and what should be the role of the board Chairman and that of the Independent Directors.

Listing Agreement specifies the requirements:

7.6 In the case of listed companies in India, Clause 49 of the Listing Agreement lays down the requirements to be fulfilled by such companies with respect to corporate governance. This clause has been successively tightened over the last few years.

---

2. See *Cadbury Committee report*, p.15.

Independent Director's Role:

7.7 The idea of having *"Independent Directors"* on the Board of Directors was conceived as a practical method for ensuring that the boards behave in a socially responsible way.

Independent Director defined:

7.8 Defining *independent director is of great practical importance.* The idea basically is to identify all those kinds of relationships which may, directly or indirectly, compromise the director`s independence. Such relationships have been identified by SEBI in a fairly comprehensive way as follows:

Independent Director is one who:

- apart from receiving director`s remuneration, does not have any material pecuniary relationships or transactions with the company, its promoters, its senior management or its holding company, its subsidiaries and associated companies;
- is not related to promoters or management at the board level or at one level below the board;
- has not been an executive of the company in the immediately preceding three financial years;
- is not a partner or an executive of the statutory audit firm or the internal audit firm that is associated with the company, and has not been a partner or an executive of any such firm for the last three years (or any legal and consulting firm having a material association with the entity);
- is not a supplier, service provider or customer of the company; and

- is not a substantial shareholder of the company, i.e. owning two percent or more of the block of voting shares.

Executive and Non-Executive Directors:

7.9 Many companies have *Executive Directors* as also *Non-Executive Directors.* The Executive Directors are whole-time employees of the companies, generally looking after a particular function. The Non-Executive Directors attend only board meetings and have no executive responsibilities. They may or may not be "Independent Directors", as some of them may be related to the promoters or have direct pecuniary interests.

7.10 Clause 49 of the listing agreement requires that at least one-half of the board should consist of independent directors in case the chairman is a promoter or is related to promoters. In other cases, at least one-third of the board should consist of independent directors. *Nominee directors* appointed by a lending public financial institution are deemed to be independent directors.

Audit Committee:

7.11 Every listed company having a paid-up capital of Rs. 5 crore or more is required to have an Audit Committee comprising at least three directors, none of whom should be an executive of the company concerned. The best practice is that the committee`s chairman should be an independent director. All members of the Audit Committee should be financially literate, i.e., have the ability to read and understand basic financial statements, such as balance sheet, profit and loss account, and statement of cash flows.

7.12 The audit committee has been given a wide mandate. It must review the annual financial statements before these are submitted to the Board of Directors. It must critically review significant adjustments arising out of audit, validity of going-concern assumption, internal control weaknesses, compliance with accounting standards and reasonability of related party transactions.

Disclosure requirements:

7.13 The disclosure requirements have been considerably tightened, specially regarding *transactions with related parties.* If any transaction is not on an arm`s length basis, the management must provide an explanation to the Audit Committee justifying the same.

Working of the independent director system:

7.14 Despite all the reforms, some problems remain. In actual working, the effectiveness of the independent director system is much less than desired.

7.15 The recent Satyam scandal indicated that the system of independent directors is not quite fool-proof. It was found that the independent directors were totally unable to stop the company`s management from indulging in fraud and deceit for nearly seven years. Not a single independent director stood up to raise a voice! As *The Financial Express* editorial of January 8, 2009 observed: "Satyam`s board of directors consisted of arguably some of the best independent directors in business . . . If such a board was unable to detect such a massive fraud and collude with poor corporate governance, what guarantee is there about other boards?"

7.16 The Satyam case has led to considerable debate about the effectiveness of independent directors, as also of the statutory auditors.

7.17 The usual reason for the ineffectiveness of the so-called independent directors is that they are most often friends of the management. That is why they were invited to be on the board. They may, therefore, find it impolite to question the management openly. They most often regard their role mainly as advisory, i.e. being a friend, philosopher and guide to the management rather than being a watch-dog. Moreover, being a director of prominent company is a matter of great prestige and is quite rewarding monetarily also.

Concluding comments:

7.18. **Assuming that an independent director is absolutely sincere, there is still the question as to how much he can know the company`s inside reality by attending the usual quarterly board meetings. There are severe limits to what he can do but his presence may often help to bring somewhat greater seriousness at board meetings.**

8

The Securities Depository System

Historical background:

8.1 The Depositories Act, enacted in 1996, was designed to introduce a demat system of holding and trading securities. The term “demat” or “dematerialisation” means paperless form, i.e., in the form of accounts only.

8.2 The first depository launched in India was the National Securities Depository Limited (NSDL). It was sponsored towards the end of 1996 by the National Stock Exchange, jointly with the IDBI and the UTI. Subsequently, in February 1999, a second depository, called the Central Depository Services Limited (CDSL) was sponsored by the Bombay Stock Exchange.

8.3 India has chosen a competitive system of depositories in order to avoid the tendency towards sloth in case of monopolies.

Depositories and Depository Participants:

8.4 The depositories operate through their agents who are known as Depository Participants (DPs). There are hundreds of depository participants dispersed all over the country. The DPs are either banks or stockbrokers.

8.5 Buying and selling of securities is now done in the form accounting entries for recording transfer from the seller`s account to the buyer`s account without the use of paper certificates. Trading in shares is now compulsorily done in demat form only. All share transactions are recorded by the DPs only. The investors have direct contact with DPs but not with the depositories.

Procedural formalities:

8.6 An investor who wants to open a depository account has to contact a Depository Participant (DP). The investor has to complete certain formalities, such as sign an Agreement Form with the DP, provide proof of identity and proof of address.

8.7 A depository account can be opened in a single name or in joint names. Nomination facility is available to the holder of depository account. This is to enable the nominee to receive the securities in case of death of the holder of a demat account. In case the securities are held jointly, different combinations of joint holders will need separate depository accounts. Different sequencing of joint holders will also require separate depository accounts.

Competitive system:

8.8 We have noted earlier that India has two competeing depositories, viz., NSDL and CDSL. Further, each of these depositories have a large number of DPs. i.e. Depository Participants who also compete among themselves.

8.9 Most DPs charge for account opening, periodical account maintenance and transactions. The DPs have been left more or less free to decide in what manner and how much they will charge to the investors for the despository services. The charges differ a great deal from one DP to another. One buys and sells shares through brokers of stock exchanges and also pay and receive the price through brokers. Many of the brokers are also DPs of either NSDL or CDSL or even both. The brokerage service is distinct and has to be paid for separately from depository service.

8.10 The DPs have to pay to NSDL/CDSL for certain services. The DPs recover this from their clients.

Transfer of an account from one DP to another DP:

8.11 A person owning securities through a Depository is the beneficial owner (BO) of the securities. As per SEBI`s decision, no charges shall be levied by a Depository on DP nor by a DP on a Beneficiary Owner (BO) when a BO transfers all the securities lying in his account to another branch of the same DP or to another DP of the same depository or another depository, provided the BO Account/s at transferee DP and at transferor DP are one and the same, i.e. identical in all respects. In case the BO Account at transferer DP is a joint account, the BO Account at transferee DP should also be a joint account in the same sequence of ownership.

Concluding comments:

8.12 Securities trading in India is now compulsorily in demat form only. The depository system has eliminated many irritating problems and costs, such as back-and-forth transmission of physical share certificates, bad deliveries, shares lost or stolen in transit, and enormous delays in registration of share transfers.

9

Investing in Mutual Funds

Convenient and economical:

9.1 A very convenient and economical way of investing in securities in through mutual fund schemes. The essential purpose behind mutual funds is to secure for small investors the benefits of diversification of risk and professional management of investments.

9.2 Mutual funds can spread their investments over scores of companies but this is not possible for a small investor. Also, most of the ordinary investors do not have the necessary skills for choosing the best possible investments nor can they devote the required time. Mutual funds resolve these problems by employing full-time professionals.

Entry load abolished by SEBI:

9.3 In order to reduce the expenses for the investor while investing in a mutual fund, the SEBI banned fund houses from charging the usual 2.25% entry load with effect from August 2009. What prompted SEBI to take this measure was that fund houses indulged in giving lavish parties and expensive gifts to distributors, extensive advertisements and countrywide road shows to sell New Fund Offers (NFOs). Now, the buyer can negotiate the commission he/she is prepared to pay to the distributing agents.

Types of Mutual Fund Schemes:

9.4 There is a great variety of mutual fund schemes. The broad types are:

(1) Equity Schemes

(2) Balanced Schemes

(3) Bond Schemes

(4) Money Market or Liquid Schemes

Within each broad category, there are sub-categories as briefly explained a little later.

Equity schemes:

9.5 The original purpose of mutual funds was to enable small investors to invest in equities. Within equity schemes, there are many types, such as:

(a) **Broadly diversified**: The fund manager decides the composition of the equity portfolio. For ensuring reasonable broad diversification, SEBI regulations require that not more than 5% of the fund should be invested in any one company.

(b) **Index Funds**: Here, the portfolio composition is not decided by the fund manager but is given by a particular index, as announced at the time of launching the scheme. Usually, it is either the NSE`s Nifty or the BSE`s Sensex. An index fund can reduce the fund management costs substantially because it does not need highly paid fund managers for selecting investments and also because it involves lower transaction costs as the portfolio does not need churning. That is why the cost of running an index fund is much lower than the cost managing a discretionary diversified equity fund. Hence, *index funds charge lower management fees and expenses to the extent of almost one-half, compared to discretionary diversified funds. Some other operational features of index funds are:*

- Some purchases and sales of stocks will be necessitated even in the case of index funds because some existing investors may leave the fund and some new investors join the fund from time to time. The purchases and sales of stocks have to be made in such a manner that the portfolio composition continues to match the index chosen. This means that if the fund has to reduce its portfolio size by, say, 1%, then each distinct holding should be reduced by 1%. The exact calculation may mean fractions of some shares but shares cannot be sold or bought in fractions. The fund manager can only try to match the fund`s portfolio to the index as nearly as possible. Slight mismatch, known as "tracking error", will generally remain but this is unlikely to affect the fund`s performance materially.

- Agencies which compile the share index usually revise the index at some intervals by replacing some of the existing companies by others. The agency has to give an advance notice to the public about such changes. The index fund will have to readjust its portfolio composition so that it corresponds to the revised index. Some changes in the composition of the index are necessitated by mergers and liquidations of companies also.

(c) **Industry–specific**: A mutual fund may specialize in particular industry segments, the idea being to concentrate on certain promising types of industries.

(d) **Mid-cap funds**: Some funds specialize in young companies of "medium-size" in the hope that they are likely to grow much faster than the big and established companies.

9.6 **Balanced schemes:** *Such schemes* invest in both equity and bonds, specifying the limits in the form of percentage to be invested in equity and bonds respectively, such as at most 60% in equities and atleast 40% in bonds. The idea is to provide a mix of equity and bonds in a single scheme.

9.7 **Bond schemes:** *Pure bond schemes*, also known as income schemes, invest in government and corporate bonds of medium and long duration. The bulk of their income arises from interest and some part from trading of bonds. Bonds are exposed to *interest rate risk.* In case the interest rates rise, the market value of the existing bond portfolio will fall. Another risk in the case of bond portfolio arises from *defaults* by the issuers. Such risk is less in the case of highly rated bonds. Also, bond schemes do not enjoy the tax advantage which equity schemes have.

Net asset value (NAV) concept:

9.8 Once a mutual fund scheme has been floated, the buying and selling prices of its units from day to day are related to the NAV of the units according to the regulations of SEBI. It is important for investors to understand the NAV concept. The following points may be noted:

Daily NAV: A mutual fund is required to compute the NAV once a day based on the closing market prices by valuing all assets and liabilities at their *current values.*

NAV per unit: The steps involved in computing the *NAV per unit* are as follows:

(a) Compute the aggregate assets of the fund *as a whole* at current values.

(b) Compute the aggregate liabilities at current values.

(c) Compute the *aggregate* NAV i.e. (a) minus (b) mentioned above.

(d) Compute the *per unit* NAV by dividing the aggregate NAV by the total number of units outstanding. That is:

$$\text{NAV of per unit} = \frac{\text{Aggregate NAV}}{\text{No. of units outstanding}}$$

9.9 **Mutual fund and stock market relationship**: *The NAV per unit of an equity fund is linked to the value of the fund`s portfolio, which, in turn, is related to the ups and downs of the stock market.* The fickleness of the equity market as a whole thus affects the mutual fund investors through its effect on the NAV per unit.

9.10 Just as investors in shares watch the share prices in order to know how their investment is faring, a mutual fund investor can keep track of the progress of the fund by looking at the movement of the NAV per unit. If the stock market crashes, the value of an equity fund will also crash. As Peter Lynch has said, "there is no such thing as a crash-proof portfolio". Even the best fund manager cannot protect the investor in such an eventuality. Short-term and cyclical fluctuations are a characteristics of stock markets all over the world.

Closed-end and open-end schemes:

9.11 Mutual fund schemes may be either (a) closed-end or (b) open-end but most of them are open-end. A *closed-end fund* has a fixed number of units outstanding, just like shares of a company. Such units are listed on stock exchanges and traded in the market at the prevailing market prices in the same way as shares of a company. The liquidity of such units depends on how actively they are being traded. With just a few exceptions, most closed-end funds are not actively traded but have a fixed tenure. At the end of such tenure, the fund is liquidated and the money returned to the unit holders. An *open-end mutual* fund has arrangement both to issue further units and also to repurchase existing units from the holders. The sale and repurchase prices are both linked to the NAV. The SEBI has laid down rules for regulating the maximum permissible spread between issue and repurchase prices of open-end schemes.

9.12 In the case of closed-end schemes, it has been observed that their market price is often significantly lower than the NAV (i.e., "at a discount to NAV", in market parlance). This has always been a puzzle because it looks illogical. In such a case, the unitholders will be better off if the fund is liquidated and the money returned to the unitholders.

9.13 **Open-end schemes are better:** From the investor`s viewpoint, open-end funds are preferable because they provide immediate liquidity to the investor in case of need. They also keep the fund`s management on its toes. If an open-end fund is poorly managed, the investors can walk out any time. This is not so in the case of closed-end schemes which, in a sense, lock-in the existing investors. In the case of actively traded closed-end funds, an existing investor can sell his holding in the market but usually at a price which is significantly below the NAV.

Future performance is the key:

9.14 A mutual fund`s future performance over the long-term is directly linked to the kind of companies in its portfolio: Are these the companies and industries in which good growth is expected over the long-term? The mutual funds are required to disclose their portfolio in periodical reports. This is to enable investors to form a broad judgment about the fund`s portfolio. There is generally a fair degree of performance continuity in the case of large, diversified and established mutual fund schemes.

Direct shareholding — some advantages:

9.15 An advantage of direct shareholding is that, over the years, the investor becomes more knowledgeable about companies, industries and the share market. On the basis of such knowledge, the investor may buy more shares of the good companies already in his/her portfolio as and when the share price dips. The shares of the laggard companies may be disposed of. This kind of investment strategy reduces the market risk by reducing the average acquisition cost of his/her shareholdings. It also improves the over-all quality of the portfolio. A portfolio of just 5-10 carefully selected companies from different industries, held for long periods of over 5 years or even 10 years, can be quite rewarding.

Narrow diversification works well:

9.16 It has been statistically proved that more than one-half of the "market risk" is eliminated by portfolios of 5 different shares; and more than two-thirds of risk is eliminated by portfolios of 10 shares.[1] "Market risk" is the risk of loss arising from the whole market falling.

---

1. See L.C. Gupta, *Rates of Return on Equities: The Indian Experience* (Oxford University Press, 1981), pp. 33-34. 'Market risk` has to be distinguished from the risk of random error or insurable risk. See Ibid., pp. 31-32.

Diversifying beyond 10 companies can reduce the remaining market risk. However, since the remaining risk is small, its elimination brings only a minor benefit. Even this is cancelled out because too much diversification makes it difficult to supervise the portfolio.

The practical angle:

9.17 From the practical angle, a more comfortable as well as more profitable strategy would be to have a combination of direct equity holdings and mutual fund equity schemes. In this way, a well-to-do investor can avoid having too many companies in his/her own portfolio.

Systematic investment plan (SIP):

9.18 A systematic investment plan (SIP) commits the investor to invest a specified amount every month (or every quarter) in the units of a fund`s equity scheme. The number of units bought each month for the investor under the plan will depend on the ruling price: fewer units are bought when the price is high, and more units are bought when price is low. This is an in-built advantage of SIPs. It averages out investor`s buying price over the entire period of holding. *The SIP resolves a dilemma often facing investors due to ups and downs in the market price.*

9.19 The monthly or quarterly amount to be invested can be as small as Rs. 500 or Rs. 1000. Mutual funds specify the schemes for which SIP is allowed by them. Some funds charge a lower entry load under SIP than for one-time investment, but others don`t make any such distinction. An exit load under SIP is charged if the investor leaves the scheme before a specific period of time.

When is SIP advantageous:

9.20 It cannot be claimed that the SIP is always more advantageous than a lump sum investment. It all depends on the course of equity prices which form the basis for computing the price of units. *If over the total period of holding, the prices have been generally declining, the SIP would cause a loss: the redemption amount (based on NAV at the end) paid to the investor for the accumulated units in his/her account would be less than the total cost. In the opposite case of rising prices, the SIP would be advantageous.*

Example:

9.21 Consider the following simplified example: Monthly investment is Rs. 1000 for the next 12 months. The amount is invested each month immediately in units of an equity scheme at the ruling price of units.

Assumption-1 (Declining Prices): The price per unit is *Rs. 16 for first 8 months* and Rs 10 per unit for last 4 months. (This is a simplification. The price for each month would ordinarily be different.) Under this assumption, against Rs. 1000 per month paid by the investor, the number of units purchased will be 500 in the first 8 months and 400 in the last 4 months. Thus the total number of units purchased over 12 months will be 900 at a cost of Rs. 12000. The redemption of the accumulated units is done always at the closing NAV. As per our assumptions, the accumulated units are 900 and will fetch only Rs. 9000 at the closing NAV of Rs. 10 per unit. The investor suffers a loss of Rs. 3000 on the total amount invested (Rs. 12000 – 9000).

Assumption-2 (Rising Prices): The ruling prices of units are reversed, being *Rs. 10 for first 8 months* and Rs. 16 for last 4 months. The number of units bought for the investor will be 800 in the first 8 months and 250 in the last 4 months. The total number of units accumulated over the 12 months will be 1050 for Rs. 12000. These 1050 units will fetch Rs. 16800 at the closing price of Rs. 16 per unit. There is a total gain of Rs. 4800 for the investor (Rs. 16800 – 12000).

9.22 The example given above brings out that the crucial factor is how the ruling price behaves over the period of SIP. In the real world, no one can predict the pattern of prices which will prevail in the future over the next 12 months or a longer period of some years. The most advantageous situation for the investor is when his/her over-all buying cost is the least and the realisable price on completion of the investment plan is the highest.

9.23 An investor, who joins the SIP at a wrong time (i.e. when the equity prices are all-time high), will be in an unfortunate situation unless the prices rise further in the future. Thus, we see that the averaging of price over the period of SIP does not always insulate the small investors against the market`s volatility.

9.24 In the case of SIP, the possibility of loss can be avoided by not starting at the wrong time (i.e. when equity prices are too high) but not many individual investors could judge the price level correctly because of its very volatile character. If we look at the movements of BSE Sensex, a significant fall or rise of 20-25% within a few months is fairly common. The SIP provides a very imperfect solution to the problem posed by market`s high volatility.

9.25 **Caution needed:** The *investor should not take it for granted that SIP is always advantageous. The price level at the starting point is particularly important,* as illustrated above. The price level at the end of the period chosen is also critical. *The rigidity of most SIP schemes can be both inconvenient and disadvantageous to the investors. The investor should avoid a situation of forced redemption of accumulated units at unduly low price by building some flexibility in the choice of redemption date.*

How the investor can overcome the disadvantage:

9.26 *The disadvantage of redemption at an unfavourable time when the prices are too low can be overcome in another way, viz, by reinvesting the redemption proceeds immediately at the prevailing low prices.*

Exchange-traded funds:

9.27 Exchange-traded funds (ETFs) are similar to mutual fund schemes, except that ETFs, as the name suggests, are listed on the stock exchanges and can be bought and sold like shares.

They were introduced in India for the first time in December 2001. The ETFs in India are based on an equity index, such as the Nifty Index and the BSE Sensex. The ETFs usually trade at a price close to the net asset value of the fund on which they are based.

9.28 Investors in ETFs need a demat account with depository participant and have to trade through a registered stock broker.

9.29 Units of mutual funds are bought and sold through the fund house at price related to the NAV (net asset value) which is declared by the concerned mutual fund only once at the end of the day. Investors who are focused on short-term price movements may like ETFs but the ETFs have no significance for long-term investors. On the other hand, most mutual fund investors are long-term investors.

Gold exchange-traded funds:

9.30 Gold Exchange-Traded Funds provide an avenue for investing in gold. Such a fund is like a mutual fund backed by gold as the underlying asset. These funds are designed to offer investors a means of owning gold without having to take physical delivery of gold. They can easily buy and sell gold units through trading on the stock exchange. They are normally quoted in price per gram of gold. This provides liquidity to the holder.

9.31 The first Gold Exchange Traded Fund was started in India in March 2007. Gold ETFs have been launched in India by Benchmark Asset Management Company, UTI Mutual Fund, Kotak Mutual Fund, Reliance Mutual Fund, Quantum Gold Fund, SBI Mutual Fund etc.

9.32 A unit of Gold ETF represents approximately one gram of pure gold in most such schemes in India. Such units are held in the investor`s demat account.

9.33 There are risks and costs in holding gold in physical form. These problems are avoided by Gold ETFs. The purity of gold is also ensured.

9.34 In India, traditionally, holding of gold jewellery as an investment has been popular, even though expensive because of charges for making and safe custody. Further, while jewellary can be passed on to one`s successors, it is not really a liquid investment and cannot be traded. Gold Exchange-Traded Fund overcomes this problem.

Money market schemes:

9.35 Money market or liquid schemes invest in money market instruments which are of very short-term maturity and, therefore, do not generally involve much interest-rate-risk. Such schemes compete with bank deposits as a method of holding liquid balances.

10

Understanding And Interpreting The Accounting Statements

10.1 The two most important accounting statements are (a) the **Income Statement,** known also as the Profit & Loss Account and (b) the **Balance Sheet** which lists the Assets and Liabilities. These statements are briefly explained below:

The Income Statement:

10.2 The Income Statement shows, on one side, the *revenues* generated from sales, as well as other sources of income, such as income from investments held by the company.

10.3 The other side of the Income Statement shows the *running expenses*, such as raw materials consumed, employee costs, power consumed, transport, communications, repairs, insurance, interest on borrowings, etc.

Top-line and bottom-line:

10.4 The two key figures to watch from the investor`s viewpoint are the *sales revenues* (*called the top line because it is shown at the top*) and *net profit (called the bottom line* because it is shown at the bottom as a residual*)*.

10.5 The primary focus of most shareholders ordinarily is on the bottom-line, i.e., the net profit. If the bottom–line disappoints the shareholders, the company`s share price is likely to be affected adversely. The bottom-line performance is of more direct concern to the investors than the top-line performance. The dividends paid by companies ordinarily depend on the net profit earned.

10.6 At the same time, it should be remembered that the bottom-line performance depends importantly on the top-line performance. The bottom-line and the top-line should be viewed in conjunction with each other for a better understanding of the company`s present situation as also its future prospects.

The *top-line growth* indicates the position which a company occupies in the market for its products and also because it constitutes the ultimate source of profits. Of importance to the investors are questions such as: Is the company a dominant player or only a marginal one? Are its sales growing? Are the costs within reasonable control allowing adequate margin for profit.

Depreciation provision:

10.7 Among the costs is depreciation which represents a reduction in the value of depreciable assets (like plant and machinery, building, vehicles, etc.) due to wear and tear. It takes the form of a percentage of the asset value. The annual depreciation provision is based on the estimated life of an asset. It does not involve any immediate cash outgo from the company. However, the asset will need to be replaced when worn out.

10.8 The annual depreciation provision is accumulated over the life of the particular assets in a "depreciation fund" which is intended to be used for replacing the worn out assets. However, a company is free to use the depreciation fund for investing in whatever way it thinks best. For example, it may like to change its line of business by investing in a new line.

Net operating income:

10.9 A company`s *net operating income* is equal to sales *minus* the operating expenses, i.e. expenses other than financing cost.

10.10. Interest paid by a company on borrowed funds is *not* an operating expense but a financing cost of the borrowed funds. For analytical purposes, the financing costs, such as interest charges, should not be included in the *operating expenses.* Different companies use different mix of loan and equity share capital for raising the required funds. While a loan involves a committed interests cost, this is not so in the case of equity capital.

Net profit:

10.11 From the net operating income we have to deduct interest charges in order to arrive at net *profit-before-tax* (PBT). From this is computed *profit-after-tax* (PAT) by deducting the income tax.

Thus, the process of computation is as follows:

Sales Revenues	*minus*	Operating Expenses
	= Net operating income	
	minus	
	Interest charges	
	= Net profit before tax (PBT)	
	minus	
	Income tax	
	= Profit after tax (PAT)	

Earning per share:

10.12 Earning-per-share (EPS) is arrived at by dividing the PAT by the number of equity shares. This is a very important figure from the investor`s point of view. The dividend-per-share (DPS) depends on the EPS.

10.13 Long-term growth in share value (as distinct from the day-to-day fluctuating share prices) depends on growth in EPS. Investor`s attempt should therefore be to identify those companies whose EPS is likely to grow relatively fast.

EPS vs. Cash flow:

10.14 Cash flow is the profit *before* charging depreciation whereas EPS is based on net profit *after* charging depreciation. Some analysts erroneously recommend the use of cash flow instead of EPS for assessing a company`s profitability. The use of cash flow can be deceptive because cash flow ignores the capital expenditure which will be necessitated for replacing worn out assets.

10.15 The PAT (profit-after-tax) is used partly for paying a dividend to the shareholders and partly for re-investing in the business.

Dividends are tax-free:

10.16 In India, the dividends in the hands of shareholders are tax-free, but the company itself is required to pay a dividend tax. The directors have to take this into account. The 'cost` to the company of paying a dividend is equal to the dividend + dividend tax.

Dividend Policy:

10.17 On an average, most of the Indian companies distribute about 25-40% of the available profit as dividend (including the dividend tax) and use the remaining profit for reinvestment. In some years, they may give an extra dividend, usually known as "special" dividend. By calling it special dividend, the companies are giving the message that the shareholders should not expect it to be repeated.

10.18 A company which pays dividends regularly and is in the habit of increasing the dividend from time to time is generally regarded very favourably by investors. In the case of well-managed companies, the normal dividend rate will be raised only if the management feels that the higher dividend can be maintained in the future. A company which is irregular in paying dividend is not liked by investors ordinarily.

The Balance Sheet:

10.19 The balance sheet shows the company`s financial position at a given point of time. It gives, on one side, the various assets of the company and, on the other side, the various liabilities arising from borrowing of money and credit purchases, as distinct from the shareholders` funds. The shareholders` funds include the share capital and the reserves built out of profits.

10.20 The term 'net worth` is frequently used for the shareholders` funds. The net worth is always equal to total assets *minus* the borrowings (i.e., total assets – borrowings = net worth). An illustration of the balance sheet is given below in percentage form in order to bring out its usual structure.

Illustration : Balance Sheet

Shareholders` Funds and the liabilities		***Assets***	
Shareholders Funds:	%	Fixed Assets:	%
(a) Share Capital			
Ordinary shares	15	Land, Building, Plant, Machinery,	
Preference shares	Nil	Furniture and Fixtures	25
(b) Reserves	20	Current Assets:	
Net Worth (a+b)	35	Inventories (stocks of finished	
Borrowings:		goods and raw materials)	40
Short term loans	10	Debtors (for credit sales, etc.)	30
Long term loans	15	Cash and bank balance	5
Creditors (for credit purchases)	40		
	100		100

The danger of excessive debt:

10.21 In the illustration given above, the total borrowings constitute 65% and shareholders` funds constitute only 35%. A question which arises is whether the company has borrowed too much and may fail to pay interest and loan instalments as per contractual terms. Such failure can land the company into serious financial trouble, specially if it is unexpectedly faced with a prolonged depression, resulting in losses. Some creditors may demand their money back. Some may file suits for recovering the money. Because of non-payment, the interest-bearing debt, such as loans taken, will begin to grow at compound interest.

10.22 A debt-free company can borrow money to tide over a difficult period but a debt-ridden company, which has defaulted, cannot easily find a lender. Many Indian companies rely on public deposits. Such companies are specially prone to financial problems because public deposits are mostly short term. Also, any default in repaying public deposits is now legally punishable.

The promoter group's key role:

10.23 A financially strong promoter group can be a source of strength for a company. Such promoters would be able to bail out the company, as they will like to save their own reputation also.

Glossary

American Depository Receipts (ADRs): An ADR represents ownership of an Indian company`s shares to be traded in the American market. The ADRs thus enable the US investors to buy shares of non-American companies without having to undertake cross-border transactions. The prices of ADRs are in US dollars. The dividends are paid in US dollars. Each ADR can represent one share or fraction of a share or multiple shares of the company concerned. The ADR system facilitates the raising of capital by Indian companies from the U.S. investors. **Global Depository Receipts (GDRs)** serve a similar purpose as ADRs for residents of various foreign countries other than the America. **Indian Depository Receipts (IDRs)** represent a recent phenomenon. They are depository receipts denominated in Indian rupees and issued in India to enable Indian residents to have a pie in the ownership of companies based abroad. Shares of such companies are listed and traded abroad but not in India. The IDRs are listed and traded on Indian stock exchanges. Thus, Indian residents can invest in rupees in foreign companies. Standard Chartered Plc is the first firm to come out with an IDR issue, offering its shares to Indians through IDRs. An IDR thus enables a foreign company to raise money in India and, at the same time, it enables Indian residents to achieve international diversification.

Arbitrage: Buying a commodity or security in one market and simultaneously selling it at a profit in another market, thus taking advantage of temporary price discrepancies.

Badla System: A system which prevailed in the Indian stock exchanges under which the buyer of shares was allowed to carry forward a trade from one settlement to the next settlement by paying badla charges (a form of interest) to those specialising in badla business. This system dominated the Indian stock market and facilitated price manipulation. It was, therefore, abolished completely in 2001.

Balance Sheet: A statement of a company`s financial position as on a given date. It lists the various assets on one side and the various liabilities plus shareholders funds on the other side.

Bond. Interest-bearing long-term securities issued by the government or companies.

Book-building: The old practice regarding share issues in India was to offer them at a *fixed price* after informally assessing the market. The old system has been replaced by a *bidding system* in which bids are invited from the investors within a stated Price Band (see below). Simply put, the bids received are arranged from the highest to the lowest in order of ranking. The issuer then finds out the *cut-off point* which will exhaust the entire issue. It determines the issue price to be charged to all investors. Those below the cut-off point would not be allotted any shares. (The actual system in India is somewhat more complicated because the applicants are categorised into Qualified Institutional Investors, Mutual Funds, Non-Institutional Bidders and Retail Individual Investors. Each category has a quota)

Basis Point: One hundredth of 1%, i.e., 0.01%.

Bulls and Bears: In market parlance, those market operators who are expecting the share prices to rise are described as bulls and those expecting the prices to decline are called bears. The market always has both bulls and bears, but some times it is dominated by bulls and some times by bears.

Capital Gain: Rise in value of a capital asset (e.g. shares) over and above the purchase price.

Capital Market: The market in which shares, bonds and other long-term securities are bought and sold.

Clearing Corporation (Clearing House): It matches, clears and settles the trades executed in the stock exchange. Now-a-days, the clearing corporation itself serves as the counter-party for every trade.

Counter-Party Risk: Every transaction in the securities market involves two parties, i.e., buyer and seller. The buyer`s obligation is to pay the price and seller`s obligation is to deliver the securities for fulfilling the contract. Counter-party risk arises if either party fails to fulfill its obligation. Such counter-party risk is now borne by the clearing corporation.

Credit Rating Agency: The credit rating system is designed to evaluate a borrower`s financial strength for repaying the money borrowed. The rating, which takes the form of symbols, is intended to indicate the probability of default by the borrower. Based on a borrowing company`s rating, the lenders decide whether to lend or not to the particular borrower and what interest rate to charge. The highest rating is AAA (pronounced as Triple A) and there is whole lot of grades below it. A critical cut-off point is between investment grades and non-investment (i.e. risky or speculative) grades. CRISIL and ICRA are India`s two leading credit rating agencies.

Dalal Street: This is the place where the Bombay Stock Exchange is located. The term has come to be used to refer to the share market in India generally.

Depreciation: Decline in the value of an asset due to wear and tear as a result of usage.

Derivatives: The term derivative means that it has no independent value. Its value is entirely derived from the value of the underlying cash asset. For example, the value of equity share derivatives is directly linked to the underlying equity shares. Similarly, the value of commodity derivatives is linked to value of the underlying commodity. Derivative contracts have fixed expiration date, mostly in the range of 3-12 months. They are used for hedging risk temporarily.

Delisting: A company may be delisted from stock exchanges if it fails to fulfil the requirements for continued listing. Sometimes a company management may voluntarily decide to get the company delisted by buying back the shares from the public.

Demutualisation of Stock Exchanges: Demutualisation of stock exchanges means the removal of stock brokers` control over the exchanges which are then run by professionals as corporate enterprises for profit, just like the other corporate businesses. Stock exchanges had been traditionally started and controlled by member-brokers as organisations mainly to serve their own members. The National Stock Exchange, sponsored by the Indian Government in 1994, was an exception. A policy decision to demutualise all the stockbroker-controlled stock exchanges was taken in 2002. This had to be done because there were rampant malpractices in the stockbroker-controlled exchanges. Many steps and legal changes were required to complete the process of demutualisation by 2007.

Dutch Auction: This is an auction system which starts with the highest bidder and goes on to successively lower bidders till the whole quantity of shares to be issued has been exhausted. The lowest accepted bid-price will then be applicable to all other successful bidders. There is no price band (i.e. maximum and minimum limits for bid price) in the auction system. The investors (bidders) are free to enter any price according to their judgement.

Efficient Market: An economic concept of a market in which the prevailing prices fully reflect all the available information and the prices adjust quickly to any new information.

Equity Shares: These represent the company`s ownership and have voting rights in the company according to the number of shares held. They are also known as ordinary shares.

Foreign Institutional Investors (FIIs): Institutional investors, such as pension funds, insurance companies, mutual funds, foundations, endowments, and many other financial institutions based abroad and registered with SEBI for portfolio investment in India.

Forward Contract: A contract between two parties for purchase/ sale of some defined commodity or securities to be delivered by one party to the other on an agreed future date and agreed terms. It is a purely bilateral contract and is not meant to be traded on an organized exchange.

Futures Contracts: These are standardized regulated contracts and are tradable on an organised exchange. Such futures contracts exist in certain commodities as well as in the stock market. Every futures contract is for a fixed period and is settled on its expiry. The holder of the contract may gain or lose, depending on the difference between the holder`s buying price and the price at the contract`s expiry. During the period of the contract, the price at which it is being traded in the market goes on changing. One may buy or sell such contracts at any time and may do so for the purpose of speculation or for hedging.

Gross Domestic Product (GDP): The value of total output of goods and services produced within a country during a year.

Global Depository Receipt (GDR): GDRs represent securities listed outside the U.S., typically in London. GDRs and ADRs (see above) basically serve the same purpose, viz. enabling companies based in developing countries, like India, to raise capital globally by issuing depository receipts which are tradable in the exchanges of the developed world.

Hedge Funds: Privately operated funds having an aggressive and quick-footed style of investing in all types of markets moving from one market to another, depending on wherever quick profits can be made.

Hedging: A technique for protecting the value of an asset by undertaking a transaction to off-set the likely fall in its value due to price fluctuations over a given period.

Inflation: The annual percentage increase in the general price level.

Initial Public Offer (IPO): The first-time issue of securities by a company to the general public.

Insider: A person, who is connected with a company`s promoter group or its management, is usually regarded as an 'insider` by reason of having access to confidential or non-public information about the company`s operations, plans, progress, problems, etc.

Insider Trading: It means trading in the shares of a company by those who have access to confidential non-public information. The insiders can make extra-ordinary profits for themselves at the cost of the unwary public. There are strict regulations prohibiting insider trading.

Listed company: It means a company whose shares are tradable on a stock exchange. Such a company has to fulfil a host of prescribed conditions intended to protect investors. Capital market regulations cover only the listed companies.

Market-Maker: A dealer who provides two-way quotes for shares or securities by being ready to buy and sell at those quotes. He earns his profit from the spread between his quotes. His presence ensures liquidity and smooth functioning of the market.

Money Market: The market for short-term credit instruments, such as treasury bills issued by the government or commercial paper issued by corporates.

Mutual Funds: These are a form of collective saving and investment scheme which invest the funds collected from investors in shares and securities. There is a large variety of mutual fund schemes run by different fund houses registered with SEBI.

Money Laundering: Using devices to transfer the illegally obtained money in order to conceal its origin.

Net Worth: This is equal to a company`s total assets minus the liabilities to outsiders, i.e., other than the shareholders.

Nifty Index: Share price index started by the National Stock Exchange of India (NSE) in November 1995. It comprises 50 largest and highly liquid stocks listed on the NSE.

Nifty Junior Index: Commenced in November 1996. It comprises the next 50 large and liquid stocks listed on the NSE.

NASDAQ: It originated in the U.S. as a device for providing trading facility for the shares of relatively small companies. It is an offspring of the NASD (i.e. National Association of Securities Dealers). The NASD dealers used to give two-way quotations (buy and sell prices) for several thousand small companies. These quotations used to be printed on Pink Sheets at the end of the day for general information. Some of the innovative companies achieved great success and began to be traded nationally. A screen-based Automated Quotation system was introduced for such companies. Thus, 'AQ` was added to 'NASD`, making it NASDAQ. It is now the second largest U.S. exchange, and internationally famous.

OTC (over-the-counter) market: A loosely organized market for securities which are not regularly traded on a stock exchange.

Order-matching trading system: In this system, investors place buy and sell orders, generally indicating the price limit for executing their order. The accumulated *buy* orders at any particular time are ranked according to the price limit (i.e. maximum buying price) which the various buyers are prepared to pay. The *sell* orders are separately ranked in order of price limit (i.e. minimum selling price) indicated by the various sellers. A buyer seeks the lowest available price while a seller seeks the highest possible price. For executing a buyer`s order, preference will be given to the lowest seller; and, for a seller`s order, preference will be given to the highest bidder. The matching system takes into account other factors also, such as quantities ordered and time-preference.

Preference Shares: These are shares which are entitled to a fixed rate of dividend and have priority over the ordinary shares, both in the distribution of profits and the repayment of capital in case of liquidation of a company. They have no voting right in the company, unless their dividend is in arrear.

Present value of an asset: Today`s value arrived at by taking into account the year-to-year stream of future cash flows and discounting such flows to the present by appropriate discount rate (interest rate).

Price Band: Companies specify a price band, i.e. the highest and lowest limits within which the investor may submit his bid price.

Primary market: The market in which the security is first sold by the issuer.

Prospectus: This refers to the offer document published by a company making a public issue of shares and/or securities. It provides details about the issue being offered to the public, together with information about the issuer, such as nature of business, risk factors, past record of business performance, etc. Details have to be given about the directors and promoters of the company, including disclosure of serious blemishes, if any, such as any criminal offence committed and punishment undergone. (See also Red Herring Prospectus)

Quote-driven trading system: A share trading system, which has market-makers (see above), giving two-way quotes, is known as quote-driven system.

Red Herring Prospectus: This term has been borrowed from the U.S. It has come to be used in India relatively recently instead of the traditional simple term Prospectus. (Herring is an eatable fish. Red herring is a type of smoked herring which is used as a bait because of its strong scent. The Prospectus also has this character because it attempts to attract investors.

Revenue: Receipts generated from sales during a given period by a commercial organisation.

Reverse Book Building: This is used in case of "share buyback" by a company, i.e. when a company wants to buy back its own shares from the public, either in order to get the company delisted from stock exchanges or because the promoters and the controlling interests wish to increase their holding in the company. Such cases use the book building process in the reverse way, i.e. beginning from the lowest bid in order to minimise the buying cost.

SEBI: See Securities & Exchange Board of India.

Secondary market: The market in which existing securities are bought and sold among investors.

Securities & Exchange Board of India (SEBI): Statutory Regulatory Authority for the capital market, created by the Indian government in 1992.

Sensex: Sensitive Index, based on share prices of 30 leading companies in India. It was started by the Bombay Stock Exchange in 1978-79 and is the oldest share index for India.

Share Buyback: When a company buys back its own shares from the public, it is known as share buyback. (See Reverse Book Building also.)

Speculation: The activity of buying and selling a commodity or financial asset usually with the aim of making quick profit from change in price.

Short-selling: This means selling shares without first owning them. In such cases, the seller has to borrow the shares from a lender till the settlement date. A short-seller wants to take advantage of the prevailing high price by selling immediately in the belief that the price will soon decline and he will be able to buy the same shares at a lower price and return them to the lender. A system of short-selling can be introduced only if there is also a system of lending and borrowing of shares.

Time deposits: Deposits made with banks for a fixed period.

Treasury Bills: Very short-term securities issued by the central Government.

Underwrite: It means undertaking to buy the whole unsubscribed part of a public issue of securities by a company, thereby providing financial support to the company. The term underwriting, is also used in the context of insurance when it means accepting liability under the insurance policy.

U.S. Securities and Exchange Commission: It is the regulatory authority for the securities market in the U.S., established under the Securities Exchange Act, 1934. It became the regulatory model for many countries around the world, including India.

Volatility: The tendency of market prices to fluctuate is termed as the market`s volatility. Volatility makes investing in shares riskier.

Wall Street: This refers to the main market for securities in the U.S.

INDEX